Runes

Origins, Evolution, Mythology, Meanings, Divination, and Magic

Matthew Leigh Embleton

Copyright ©2020 Matthew Leigh Embleton. All rights reserved.

Runes

1. Origins and Evolution 1
   - 1.1. Elder Fuþark 5
   - 1.2. Gothic Fuþark 6
   - 1.3. Anglo-Saxon Fuþorc 7
   - 1.4. Marcomannic Runes 8
   - 1.5. Younger Fuþark (Long Branch) 9
   - 1.6. Younger Fuþark (Danish) 10
   - 1.7. Younger Fuþark (Short Twig Runes) 11
   - 1.8. Younger Fuþark (Hälsinge Staveless Runes) 12
   - 1.9. Younger Fuþark (Orkney) 14
   - 1.10. Younger Fuþark (Manx-Jeran) 15
   - 1.11. Younger Fuþark (Twig Runes) 16
   - 1.12. Younger Fuþark (Tent Runes) 18
   - 1.13. Icelandic Fuþark 20
   - 1.14. Greenlandic Runes 21
   - 1.15. Medieval Runes 22
   - 1.16. Dalecarlian Runes 23
2. Mythology 24
3. Meanings 32
4. Divination 51
5. Magic 57
6. Bindrunes 64
7. Runic Inscriptions 81
8. The Misuse of Runes: What to Avoid 87

Cover: Three sets of runes, photo by the author.

Acknowledgments

I have long been fascinated by languages and history, and I am very grateful to the special people in my life who have supported and encouraged me in my work. Thank you for believing in me. You know who you are.

Introduction

In such times of increasing misunderstanding, incomplete information, misinformation, and misguided criticism, it has become necessary to add a number of clarifications in order to set the record straight in this expanded introduction.

The Viking Age and North Germanic Paganism

In recent decades popular culture has rediscovered the Viking Age and North Germanic Paganism with fresh eyes. From the pirates and sea raiders known as Vikings, to the fierce warriors called Berserkers, and the wider Norse or Nordic people as a whole, symbols played an important role in daily life and spirituality.

Today we find these symbols visually eye catching and their meanings fascinating. People all over the world are finding meaning in these symbols that resonate with their personality, identity, and spiritual beliefs.

Symbols for personal magic

These symbols are a representation of a thought or an idea, from a single line to an ever increasingly complex symmetry of lines, circles, intersecting lines, and bold striking angles. Perhaps one of the most popular of these symbols is the Vegvísir, one of the many Galdrastafir (praying or chanting staves) that appeared in Iceland after its settlement by Norse people in the late 9th century, but there are many many more.

Runes

The meaning of the word 'rune' comes from the Germanic root '*run-*' meaning '*secret*' or '*whisper*'. Similar versions of this word are also found in Old Irish Gaelic, Welsh, Old English (Anglo-Saxon), Baltic languages such as Lithuanian, and also Finnish, with such meanings as '*intention*', '*miracle*', '*mystery*', '*poem*', '*scratched letter*', '*secret*', '*secret writing*', '*speech*', '*to carve*', '*to speak*', and '*whisper*', which collectively suggest a common connection over a broad spectrum of meaning reaching far back into time. These runes are the basic building blocks of meaning which can either be used on their own, or configured into bindrunes.

Bindrunes

A bindrune or '*bindrúna*' (plural = bindrunes '*bindrúnir*') is a combination of two or more runes into a single symbol, by varying degrees of overlapping and symmetrical configuration, to compound and amplify meaning and significance. It can be used to either exaggerate or obscure the meanings of the symbols used.

Bindrunes are mentioned in the *Sigrdrífumál* which is part of the Poetic Edda (overlapping two Tyr runes and carving them on to a sword for victory). The Poetic Edda is one of the most important documents of Old Norse religion and mythology, which is known to have formed at least as far back as the Proto-Norse period (2nd to 8th centuries CE), preserved in the Codex Regius during the 1270s.

Bindrunes have been adopted by many modern traditions, revivals of traditions, syncretic traditions, religious movements, and occultist Western esoterica, including Wicca, but they are neither owned nor govered by any of them.

A large number of simple bindrunes have been popularised and widely disseminated into these modern traditions in many circles. They have been carved, burned, engraved, or even printed on to all manner of personal items by craftspeople all over the world, and such items are a valuable introduction into the idea of personal talismanic magic.

These popular bindrunes are included in this book as reference, but they are by no means the only ones available, and to describe them as being 'wicca' in nature is incorrect. They are part of an ancient tradition and they exist by invention and for the purpose of invention, through the creativity of the individuals who formulate them and use them.

As well as considering the design of these bindrunes, the reader is also encouraged to consider formulating their own personal bindrune or bindrunes, using the runes as building blocks, using the basic principle of symmetry described in this book or not, as is their personal choice.

The misuse of symbols

Galdrastafir have been associated with the misuse of runes and Norse symbols as a whole. In 2019 reports emerged claiming that depictions of runes and Norse symbols, including those represented in traditional Viking jewellery, may soon be banned in Sweden, including *Mjolnir* (Thor's Hammer), the *Valknut*, and the *Vegvísir* ('way-seer' / 'way marker' / Nordic compass).

For the last 120 years, runes and other Norse symbols have been misguidedly misused, misrepresented, and misinterpreted by some, as part of systems of propaganda for extreme and objectionable political agendas. This form of cultural appropriation has done great damage in obscuring and twisting the original and true meanings of the runes.

The misuse of runes by the Nazis is well documented and well known, but sadly this knowledge is sometimes inadvertently misused by people who in their noble fight against objectionable political ideas and their association with historical atrocities end up losing their way, equating this misuse of runes with that of a 2,000 year old tradition which is experienced innocently by pagans and spiritualists around the world, who have been mistakenly and undeservedly reviled as being associated with ideas and beliefs that they do not have and find abhorrent as much as the next person.

The 'Othala' or 'Odal' rune

One particular example is the 'Othala' or 'Odal' rune, which is perhaps the easiest of runes to have its meaning distorted in this way since it represents the idea of ancestry and homeland. There are two versions of this symbol, one with 'feet' or 'wings' and one without. The version without these 'wings' or 'feet' is the older of the two and is found in the majority of Futharks.

The version with 'wings' or 'feet' comes from its traditional use as a regular pattern of interlocking Othala runes, the right way up and upside down contiguously, around the circumference of property, such as the wall of a house, or a fence around a piece of land.

This version of the rune has also been used as an astrological symbol for Asteroid #3989 known as 'Odin' discovered on 8th September 1986 by P Jensen at the Brorfelde Observatory in Denmark. The name and number of this asteroid was allocated by the Minor Planet Center (MPC) which is part of the Smithsonian Astrophysical Observatory. All of this has been overlooked in favour of the idea that it was exclusively used by the Nazis.

A clear difference in the Nazi use of the 'Othala' or 'Odal' rune along with the rest of the runes is the bold, thick, and lines with thick squared corners, rather than the thin lines that one would normally see in runes that are carved or written.

Perhaps the most difficult way of innocently representing this rune would be in the form of a pendant in which the rune appears on its own without any backing, since a degree of thickness would be needed in order to provide rigidity and durability to avoid it being bent or broken. There are anecdotal accounts in discussion forums on the internet describing how people have punitively snatched such pendants from around the necks of wearers exclaiming "Nazis wear these!"... to which the correct answer must be... "*...and so do millions of innocent pagans!*".

Hate symbols

The Anti-Defamation League has an online database of hate symbols containing runes misused by Nazis and far-right groups, rightly stating that because these runes continue "to be used by non-racists, typically adherents of neo-pagan religions, one should not simply assume that a particular use of this symbol is racist, but should carefully judge it in its context".

Conclusion

By discovering these magical symbols, you are rightly reaffirming the true meaning of their culture. Not only that but in true spirit you are refusing to allow access to this culture to be denied to you by those who mistakenly believe that the misuse of these symbols is their only use. Such people seeking to revile and punish innocent users of pagan symbols are actually enabling far right organisations to steal this culture.

The magic of the Norse people worked because they believed that it worked. They believed in the process of signalling and communicating their intentions and desirable outcomes to the forces around them, projecting them into the universe, and having the confidence and belief to make things happen.

1. Origins and Evolution

The meaning of the word 'rune' comes from the Germanic root *'run-'* meaning *'secret'* or *'whisper'*. Similar versions of this word are also found in Old Irish Gaelic, Welsh, Old English (Anglo-Saxon), Baltic languages such as Lithuanian, and also Finnish, with such meanings as *'intention'*, *'miracle'*, *'mystery'*, *'poem'*, *'scratched letter'*, *'secret'*, *'secret writing'*, *'speech'*, *'to carve'*, *'to speak'*, and *'whisper'*, which collectively suggest a common connection over a broad spectrum of meaning reaching far back into time.

The first known account of the use of runes as a means of divination is attributed to Publius Cornelius Tacitus in his work 'De Origine et situ Germanorum' (On the Origin and Situation of the Germanic People) of around 98 C.E.

> *"Auspicia sortesque ut qui maxime observant: sortium consuetudo simplex. Virgam frugiferae arbori decisam in surculos amputant eosque notis quibusdam discretos super candidam vestem temere ac fortuito spargunt".*

> "They attach the highest importance to the taking of auspices and casting lots. Their usual procedure with the lot is simple. They cut off a branch from a nut-bearing tree and slice it into strips, these they mark with different signs and throw them at random onto a white cloth".

While it gives no specific description of the signs or symbols used, the description of the process of casting lots makes it probable that the symbols being used were an early form of runes.

During the Roman Imperial period (1st century B.C.E. to 5th Century C.E.) Germanic people would have had contact with the Roman Empire through trade and also by serving as mercenaries in the Roman Army. They would have come into contact with and adopted writing systems from Old Italic alphabets, including Venetic, East Raetic, West Raetic, Camunic, Lepontic, and Etruscan . The fact that these alphabets share so many common features makes it hard to determine whether one specific alphabet was the point of origin, or a combination of them.

Either way, this can be said to be the historical 'fork in the road' where runic alphabets and the Latin alphabet began their development and went their separate ways.

The word 'alphabet' itself comes from the Greek 'alpha' + 'beta', the first two letters in the sequence. Likewise, the runic alphabets will hereafter be referred to as 'Futharks' or 'Fuþarks' in the same way, because of the first six letters 'F', 'U', 'Þ', 'A', 'R', 'K'.

Here it is worth noting the existence of two extra letters: The 'Þ / þ' letter known as 'Thurisaz' or 'thorn' represents the unvoiced 'th' sound as in 'think'. The letter 'Ð / ð' known as 'Eth' represents the voiced 'th' sound as in 'the'. Both of these letters were used in Old English (Anglo-Saxon) but began to fall out of use after the Norman invasion of England in 1066, and the subsequent evolution from Old English to Middle English from the influence of Anglo-Norman French.

They did however continue to be used in dialects of Middle English outside of London and the South-East of England as late as the end of the 14th century and beyond. One example of this is the original manuscript of 'Sir Gawain and the Green Knight' in the North West Midland dialect.

These letters were also used in Gothic, Old Norse, Old Swedish, and are still in use in modern Icelandic, arguably the closest linguistic ancestor to Old Norse. They appear frequently in the names of some of the runes.

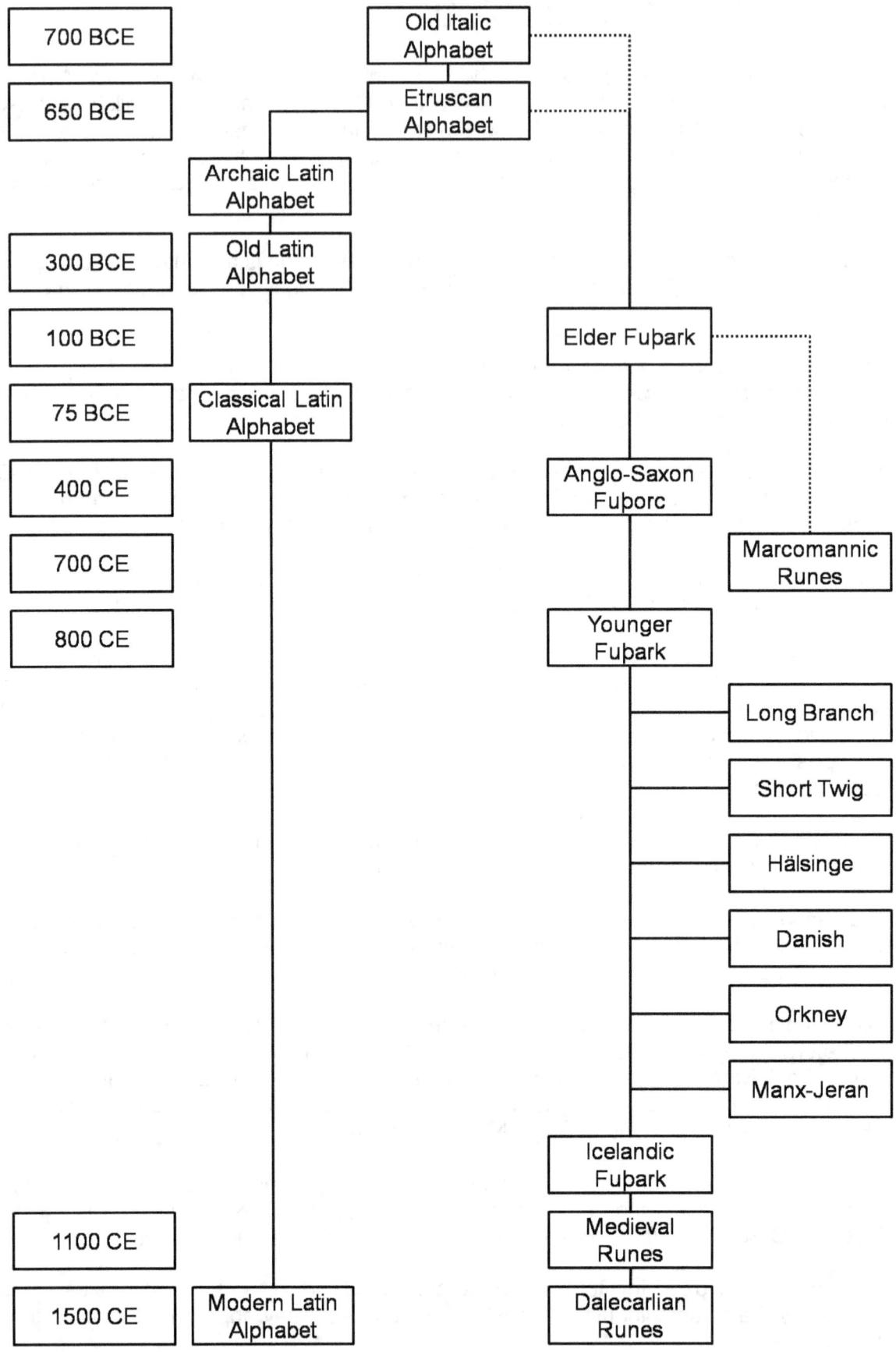

A timeline of alphabets relative to Old Italic, Runic alphabets, and the Latin alphabet

The shape and form of the runes was ideal for carving into wood or stone, owing to the straight lines rather than curves.

They were used to demonstrate ownership of personal items, who they were made by, and who they were made for.

They were also used on specially erected rune stones which acted as way markers or public notices, telling people passing by who owned the land they were on, or commemorated significant events that had taken place there.

In the evolution of formal and informal, there were a number of innovations which allowed for shortening of lines making the runes easier to carve, or also to encode runes to hide their meaning to anyone except the greatest rune masters.

One of the reasons for the evolution of the runes was the change in the languages that the runes were developed to codify.

Shifts in pronunciation of vowels and consonants across the Germanic world changed both how they were heard, and how they were transcribed.

Spelling was not standardised at the time, which meant that shifts in spelling, and in some cases missing letters (because of well known abbreviations) could be accommodated and worked around by lateral decoding while reading aloud.

Regional variations of the language had begun to evolve away from each other in their own different directions with different neighbouring influences via trade, etc.

From sharing a common Proto-Germanic root, there became a West Germanic and a North Germanic branch.

From the West Germanic branch evolved Old English (Anglo-Saxon), while the North Germanic branch became Old Norse, which split into Old West Norse, Old Gutnish, and Old East Norse.

The migration of the Norse peoples from the Old West Norse speaking areas to the settlement of Greenland brought about a unique Greenlandic Norse, which became extinct when the Norse settlement of Greenland lost contact with their neighbours and disappeared from record in the early 15th century.

Norse settlers in the Northern Isles (Orkney and Shetland) and Caithness came to speak what was known as 'Norn', which became extinct in the mid 19th century.

Old West Norse became modern Icelandic, Faroese, and Norwegian.

Old Gutnish became modern Gutnish.

Old East Norse became modern Danish and Swedish.

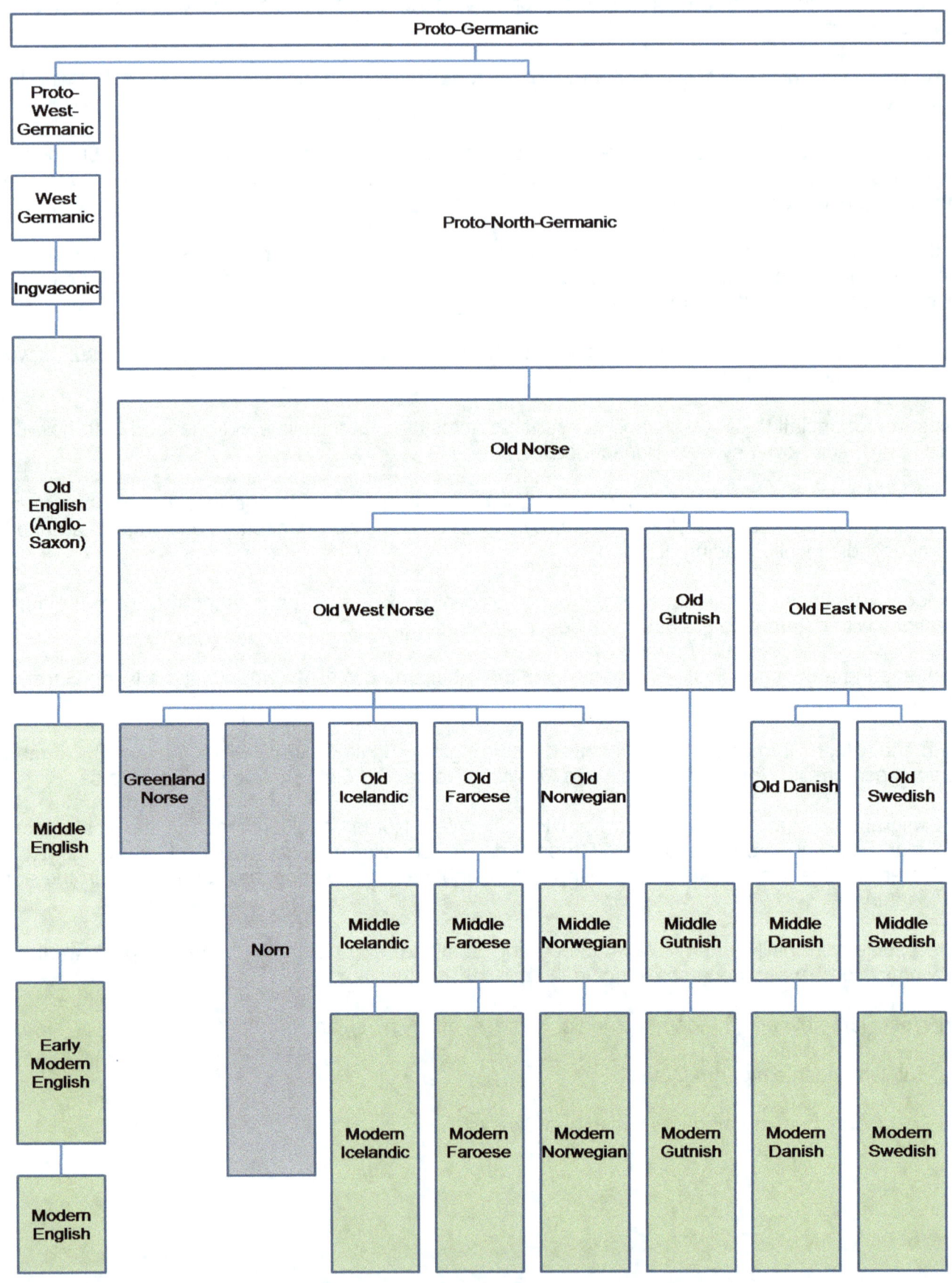

A relative timeline of Germanic languages

1.1. Elder Fuþark

Freyja's Ætt: Fehu, Uruz, Þurisaz, Ansuz, Raido, Kaunan, Gebo, Wunjo

Hagal / Heimdallr's Ætt: Hagalaz, Naudiz, Isaz, Jeran, Ihwaz, Perþo, Algiz, Sowilo (1), Sowilo (2)

Týr's Ætt: Tiwaz, Berkanan, Ehwaz, Mannaz, Laguz, Ingwaz (1), Ingwaz (2), Oþala, Dagaz

The Elder Fuþark is the first of the known runic alphabets with 24 runes arranged in three rows of eight referred to as Ætt (singular) or Ættir (plural), meaning 'groups' or 'generations'. The names of each rune are Proto-Germanic and have been reconstructed based on the names of subsequent fuþarks. There are two versions of 'Sowilo' and 'Ingwaz' that are commonly found in inscriptions, both of which are included here. While we can date the origin of the Fuþarks back to the 1st century B.C.E. the first known sequence listing all of the runes is found on the Kylver Stone which was discovered in 1903 in Gotland, Sweden, and dates back to approximately 400 C.E. so it is possible to conclude that by this time the Elder Fuþark was fully formed as we know it.

The Kylver Stone, Gotland, Sweden
(Source: Wikipedia Creative Commons)

1.2. Gothic Fuþark

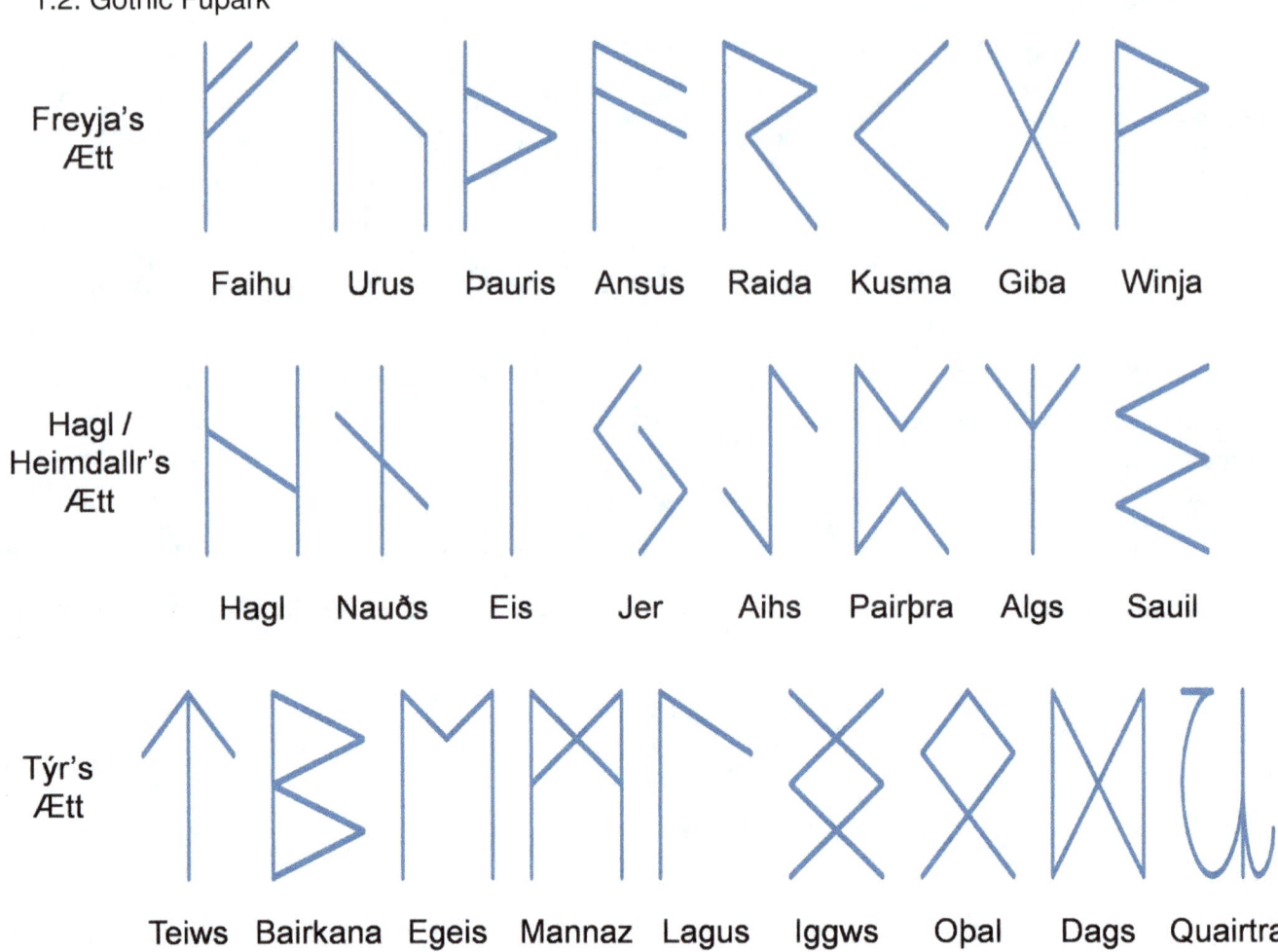

Among the East Germanic peoples, one of the East Germanic languages that we know of through surviving texts is the Gothic language spoken by the Goths.

According to the Gothic Eastern Roman historian Jordanes in his 'De Origine Actibusque Getarum' (The Origin and Deeds of the Goths) written in 551 C.E. based on the lost works of Cassiodorus, the Goths originated in Scandinavia in 1490 B.C.E. however this is debated among scholars.

The Gothic language saw a replacement of the use of runes in favour of the Gothic Alphabet in the 4th century, and the language continued being spoken in some parts of the Crimea until the 17th century when it became extinct.

The symbols are the same as the Elder Fuþark with Gothic variations on the reconstructed Proto-Germanic names for the runes, except for the addition of a 25th rune called 'Quairtra', which is believed to be an ancient symbol for fire, flame, and transformation, similar in meaning to the Anglo-Saxon rune 'Cweorth'.

'Quairtra' is a unique and enigmatic character found only in the Codex Vindobonensis 795, a 9th-century manuscript that preserves the list of Gothic runes. It is not attested in any known inscriptions, and its function and phonetic value are still uncertain.

1.3. Anglo-Saxon Fuþorc

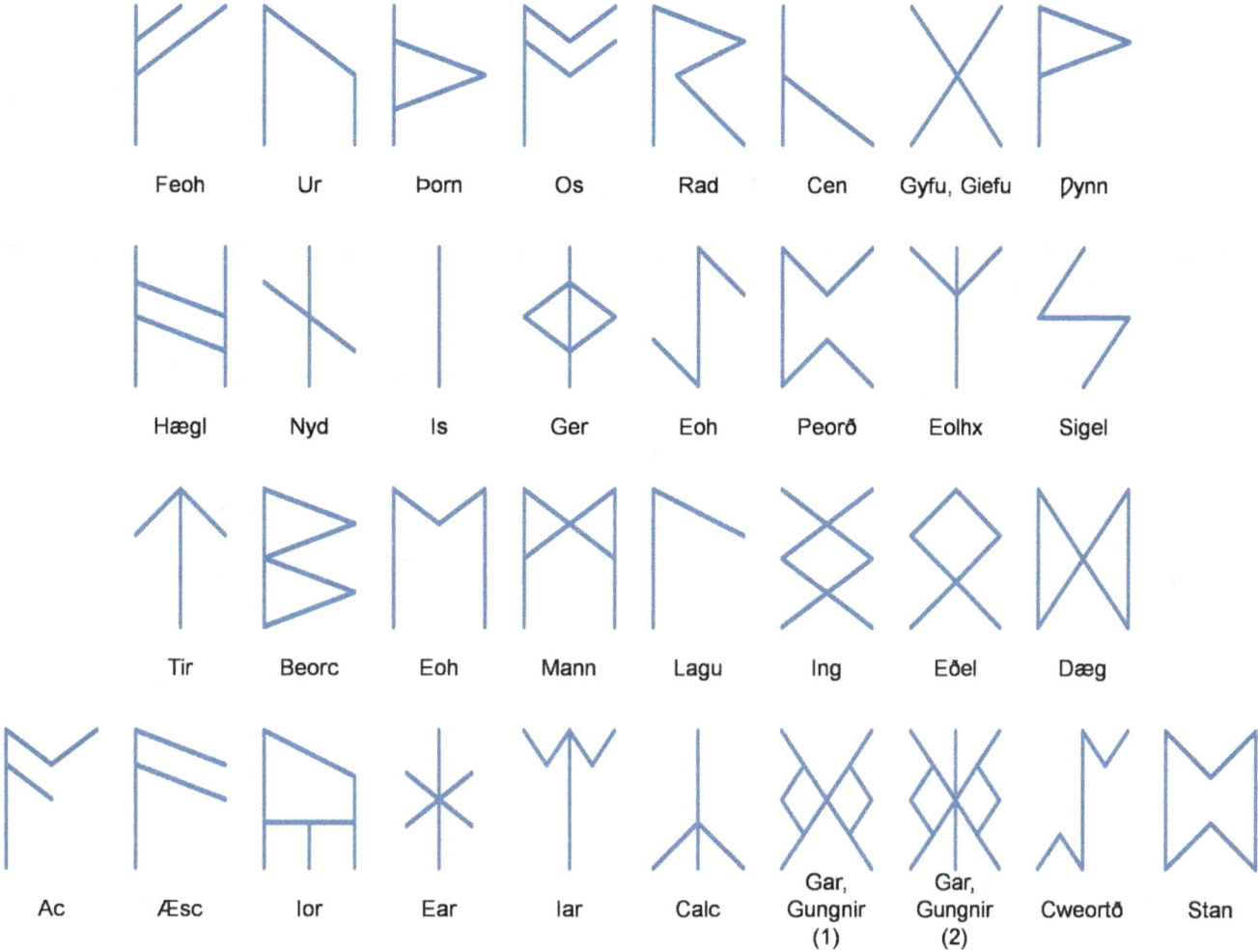

The Anglo-Saxon Fuþorc, sometimes called the Anglo-Frisian Fuþorc, is an expansion of the Elder Fuþark from 24 runes to up to 33 depending on variations, recording the Old English language of the Anglo-Saxons, which is a West Germanic language.

Part of the original expansion included variations of long and short vowels which had evolved since the Elder Fuþark was developed. For example, ᚠ becoming ᚠ āc, ᚠ æsc and ᚠ ōs.

Our knowledge of the sequence and meanings of these runes comes from the Anglo-Saxon Rune Poem, believed to have been written in West Saxon in the 8th or 9th century. This also informs the meaning of the Elder Fuþark and Younger Fuþark runes in divination and runelore.

Although it had begun to be replaced by the Old English Latin alphabet around the 7th century, knowledge of the runes was still widely known up until the 12th century

Anglo-Saxon use of runes persisted in pagan and folk traditions, but became increasingly marginalised and viewed with suspicion by Christian authorities. They occasionally appeared in charms, amulets, and cryptic inscriptions, reflecting lingering cultural or spiritual associations rather than widespread literacy.

1.4. Marcomannic Runes

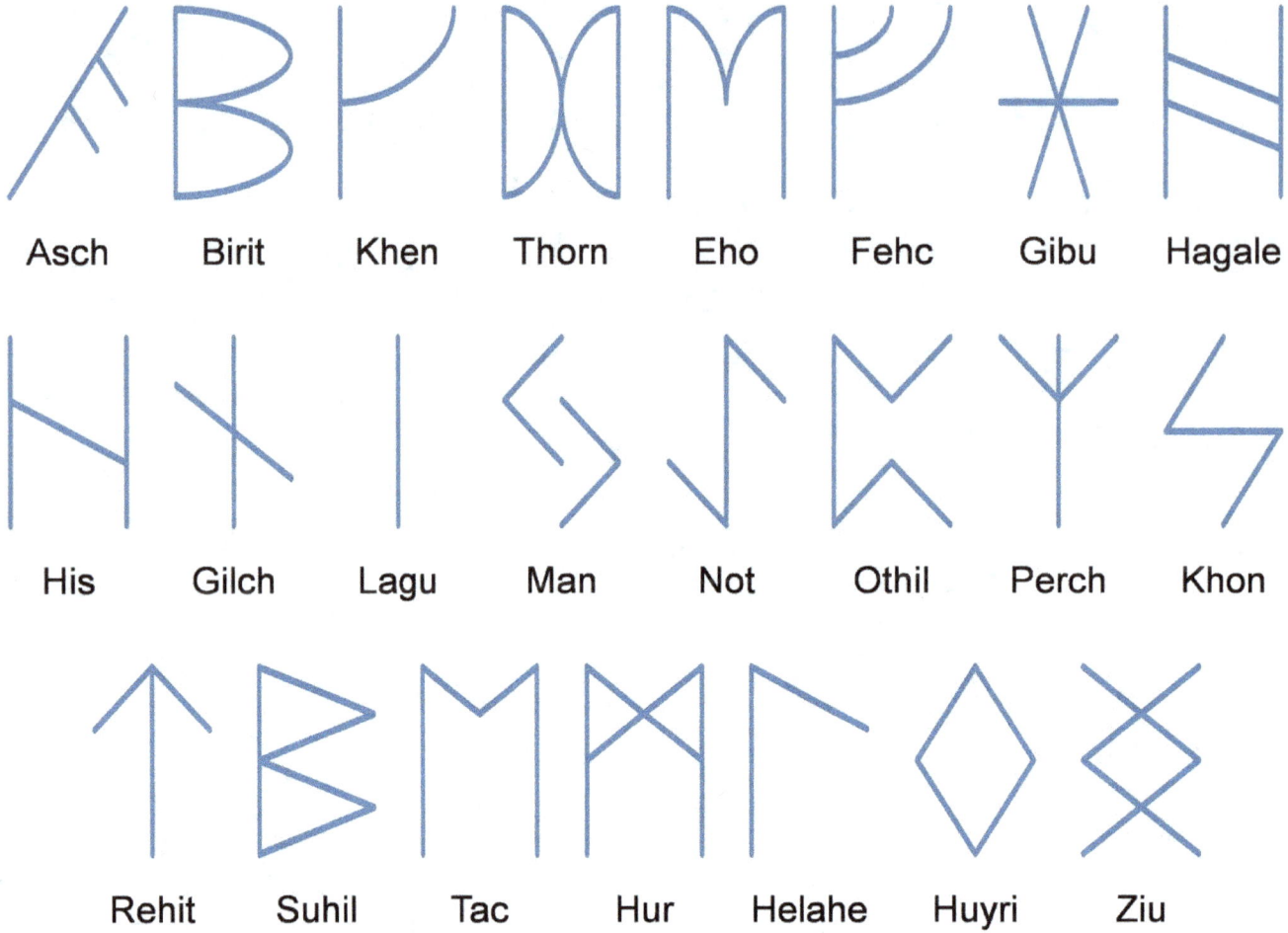

The Marcomannic runes appear to be a mixture of Elder Fuþark and Anglo-Saxon Fuþorc runes recorded in 'De Inventione Litterarum' (The Invention of Letters), a 9th-century manuscript believed to have been authored by Hrabanus Maurus, a prominent Carolingian scholar and theologian.

The work sought to catalogue and interpret various alphabets, both classical and contemporary, with the goal of illustrating the divine or philosophical origins of written language. Hrabanus seems to have attempted to represent all the letters of the Latin alphabet using runic equivalents, possibly for educational or symbolic purposes.

The runes were attributed to a Germanic tribe called the Marcomanni, but this attribution is now widely regarded as incorrect. The Marcomanni, an early Germanic people, were falsely equated in the manuscript tradition with the Nordmannos (Northmen). This is likely to have come from a misunderstanding of tribal identities or from the tendency in medieval scholarship to generalise about so-called 'barbarian' cultures.

There is no historical or archaeological evidence that the Marcomanni ever used runes, let alone this particular alphabet. The so-called Marcomannic runes are now understood to be a scholarly invention rather than a genuine writing system in active use.

The characters combine elements of known runic alphabets with the Latin script. No inscriptions or artifacts bearing these runes have been discovered. The Marcomannic runes remain a fascinating example of medieval scholarly creativity rather than a true epigraphic tradition.

1.5. Younger Fuþark (Long Branch)

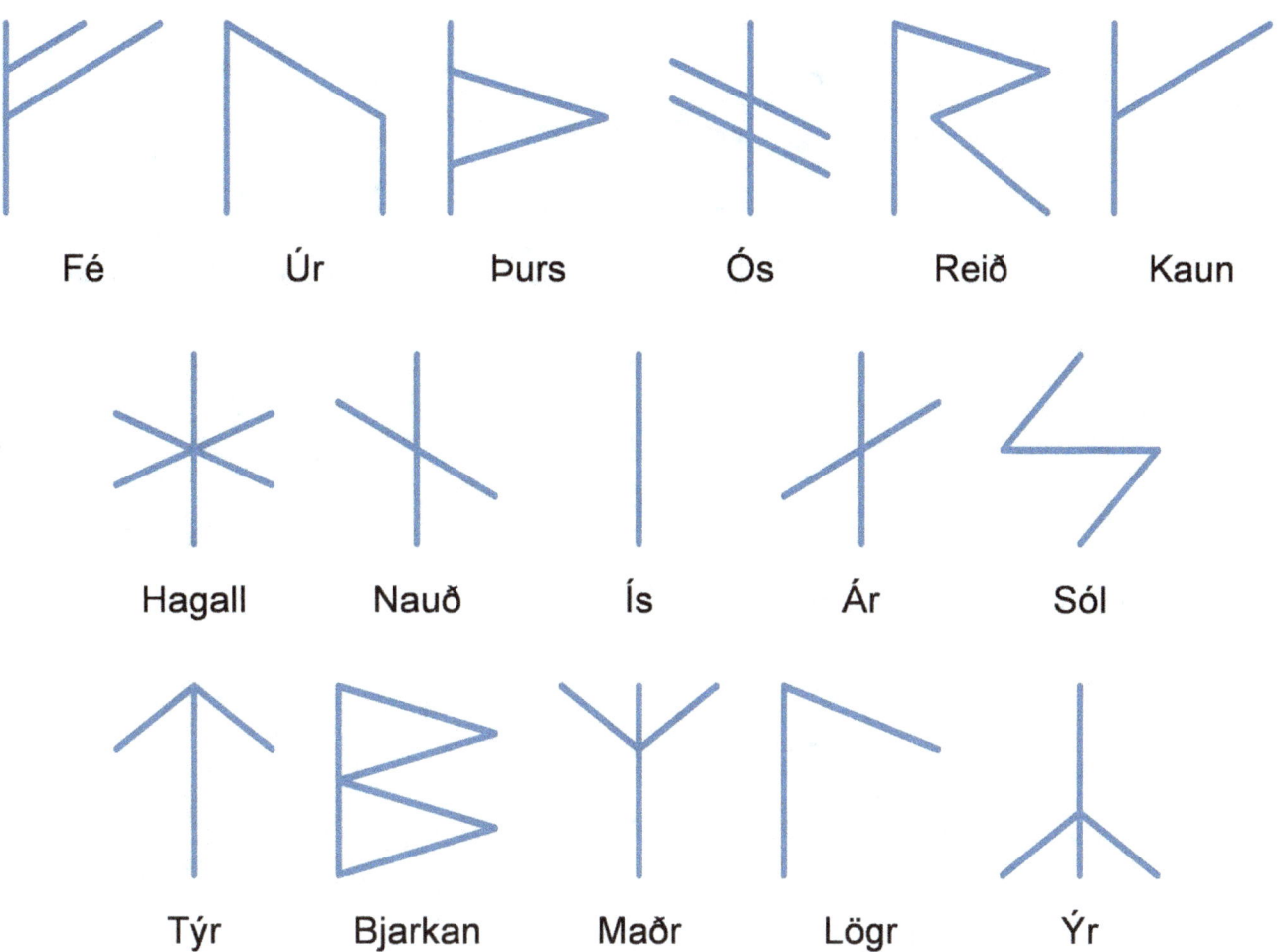

Fé	Úr	Þurs	Óss	Reið	Kaun
Hagall	Nauð	Ís	Ár	Sól	
Týr	Bjarkan	Maðr	Lögr	Ýr	

Sometimes all of the runes are collectively referred to as 'Viking Runes', but it is the Younger Fuþark that coincides with the Viking Age, and the transition of Proto-Norse into Old Norse. The Younger Fuþark is a simplification of the original 24 runes of the Elder Fuþark into 16 runes. Spelling was not standardised, sometimes letters were left out, and one rune could have several different associated sounds.

ᛒ	B / P		ᛁ	I / E / Æ / J
↑	D / T		ᚢ	U / V / O
ᚴ	G / K			Y / Ø / W
ᚡ	F / V		ᛏ	A / Æ
þ	Þ / Ð		ᚠ	A / O / Ö

The Long Branch variety (sometimes referred to as being Danish) is believed to be the original and formal version of the Younger Fuþark used in inscriptions on stone to honour the dead, indicate the wealth and authority of those who erected the monuments. Inscriptions also proclaim family relationships, inheritance rights, authority and property claims

1.6. Younger Fuþark (Danish)

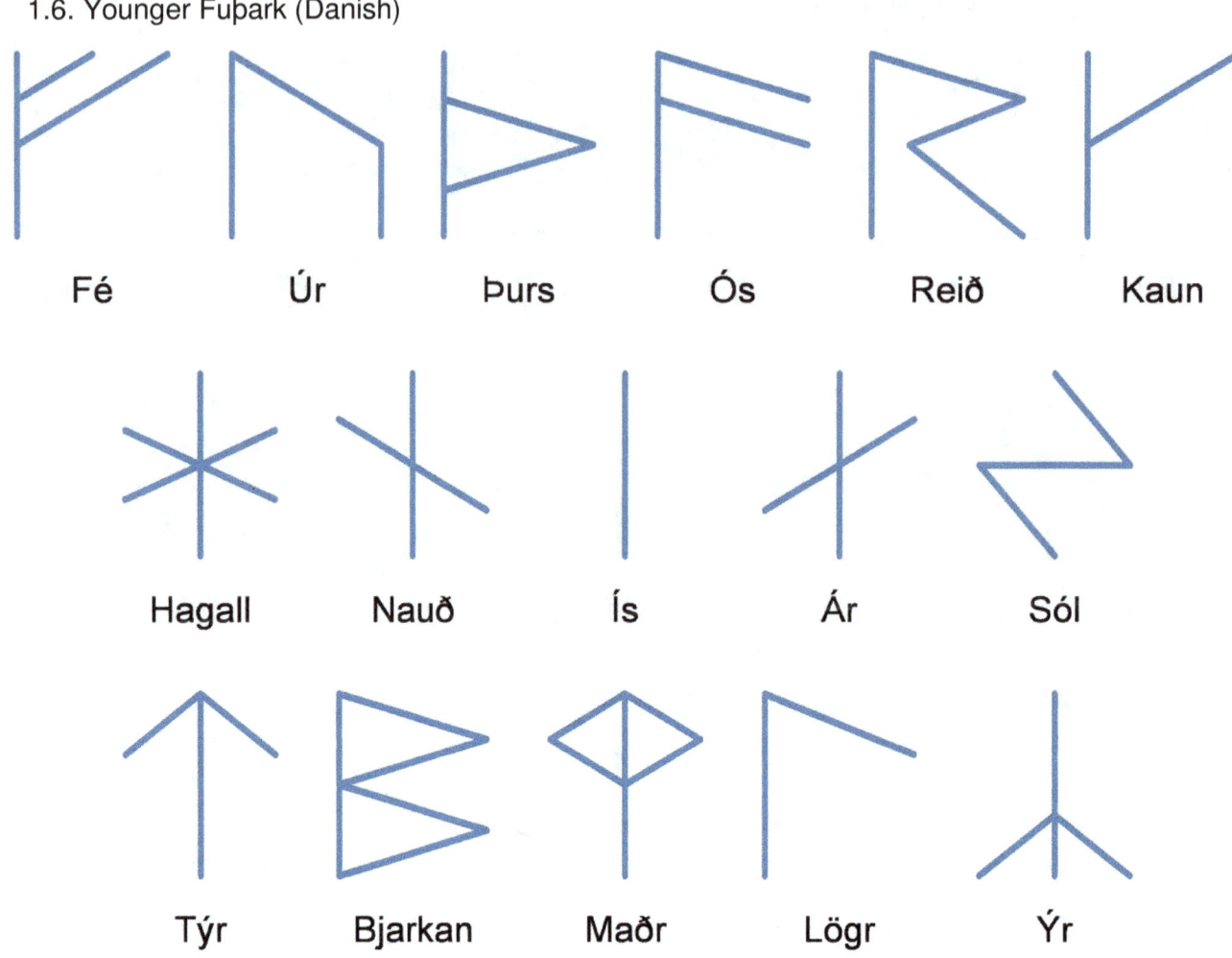

The terms 'Long-branch Younger Futhark' and 'Danish Younger Futhark' are often used interchangeably, but there are some differences. Similar to the Long Branch variety of the Younger Fuþark, this version contains variations of Ós, Sól, and Maðr

Long-branch Younger Futhark is a more general term, which refers to the elongated, formal variant of the Younger Futhark. It was primarily used for monumental inscriptions like rune stones. While most common in Denmark, it was also used in parts of Sweden and Norway for formal or public inscriptions.

Danish Younger Futhark is a more regional term, which refers to a regional and chronological variant of the Younger Futhark used in Denmark, especially from the 8th to 10th centuries.

Early Danish Younger Futhark often uses the Long-branch form, but it also shows unique rune shapes and local variations over time. It was used in Denmark and Danish-controlled areas, including parts of England (Danelaw). It represents a specific evolution of the Younger Futhark within Danish territory, not just a stylistic form.

1.7. Younger Fuþark (Short Twig Runes)

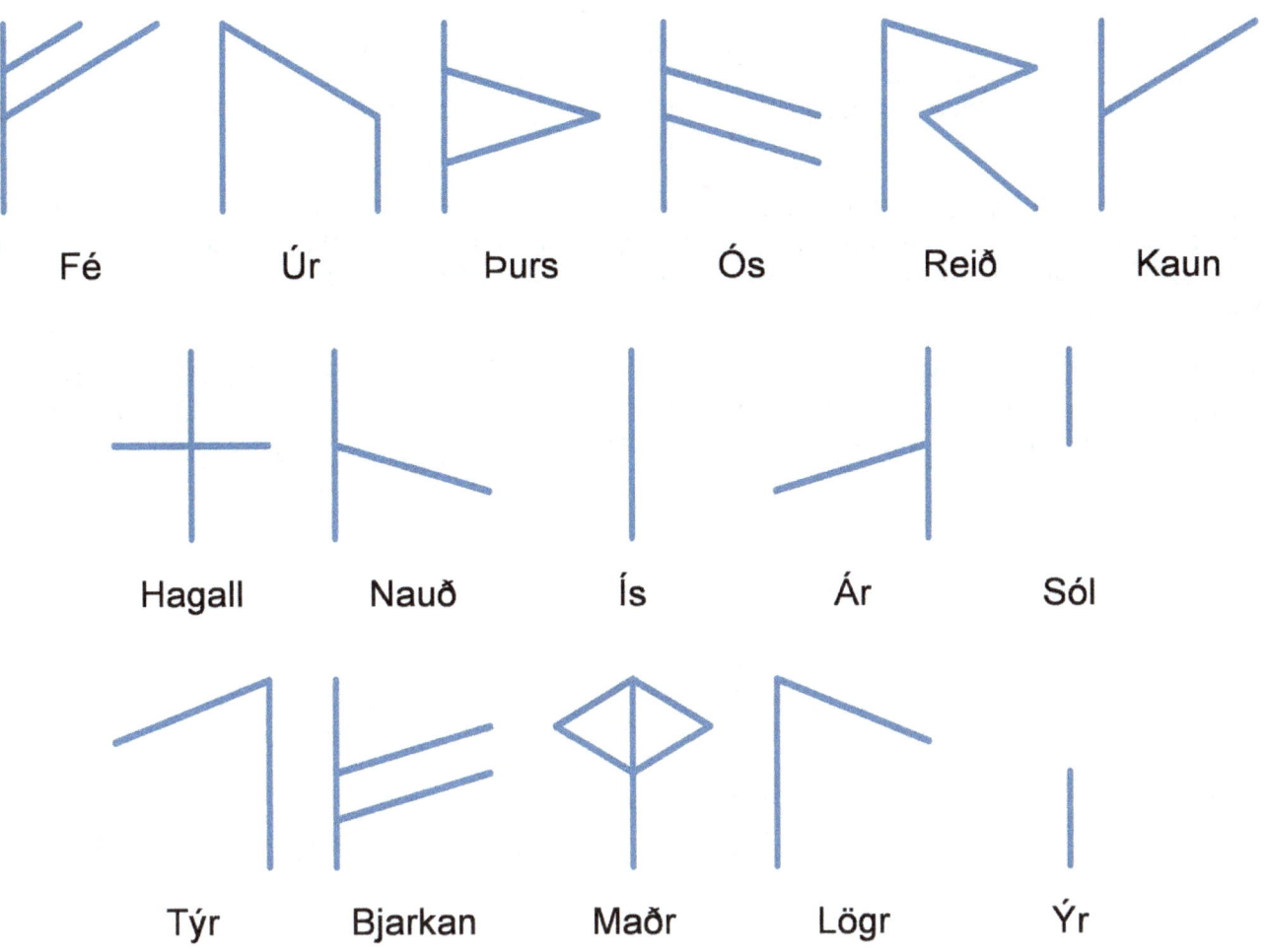

The Short Twig variety of the Younger Futhark, often associated with Swedish and Norwegian regions, features notably simplified rune shapes that facilitated easier and faster carving. This made the script especially well-suited for engraving on a wide array of everyday objects, including jewelry, weapon components, knives, spearheads, swords, coins, boxes, containers, as well as materials like bone, wood, and spindles.

The reduced complexity of these runes allowed craftsmen and users to inscribe messages or symbols quickly, even on small, curved, or irregular surfaces where more elaborate forms would have been impractical.

Because of this practicality, the Short Twig runes gained widespread popularity for informal communication and personal use among Norse populations. They served as a versatile tool for marking ownership, crafting memorials, or conveying short messages on portable items.

In contrast to the Long-branch runes, which were more decorative and predominantly used for official or monumental inscriptions such as rune stones, the Short Twig style embodied a more modest, functional approach to writing in daily life.

1.8. Younger Fuþark (Hälsinge Staveless Runes)

Hälsinge or Staveless runes are so called because they were first discovered in the Hälsingland region of Sweden. Believed to have been used between the 10th and 12th centuries, they were the logical conclusion of the simplification and minimalism of the Younger Fuþark for ease of everyday use.

Unlike typical runes, these runes lack the main vertical stroke ('staff' or 'stave') which is normally their defining feature. Instead, they are composed of only the smaller branches or strokes that usually attach to the stave, making them highly abbreviated and often difficult to read, like a kind of shorthand.

Ruled Hälsinge Staveless Runes are inscribed on surfaces where the carver first drew horizontal or vertical guide lines (rules) to help align and space the runes evenly. These ruled inscriptions appear more orderly and structured, making the runes easier to read and the overall text more uniform.

Ruled

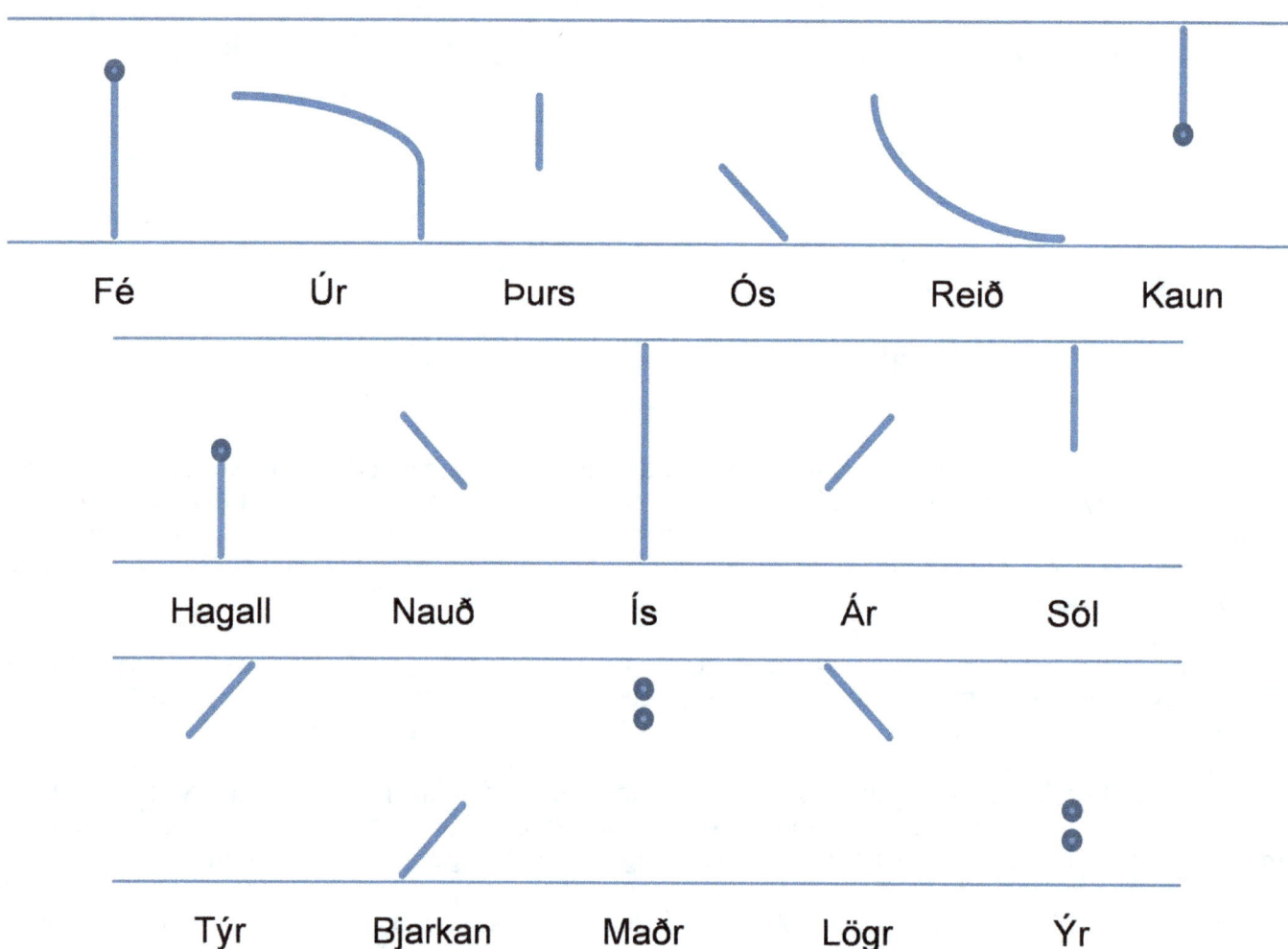

Unruled Hälsinge Staveless Runes lack such guiding lines, resulting in a more irregular, less evenly spaced arrangement of runes. These inscriptions often appear more spontaneous or informal and can be harder to decipher due to their inconsistent layout.

Unruled

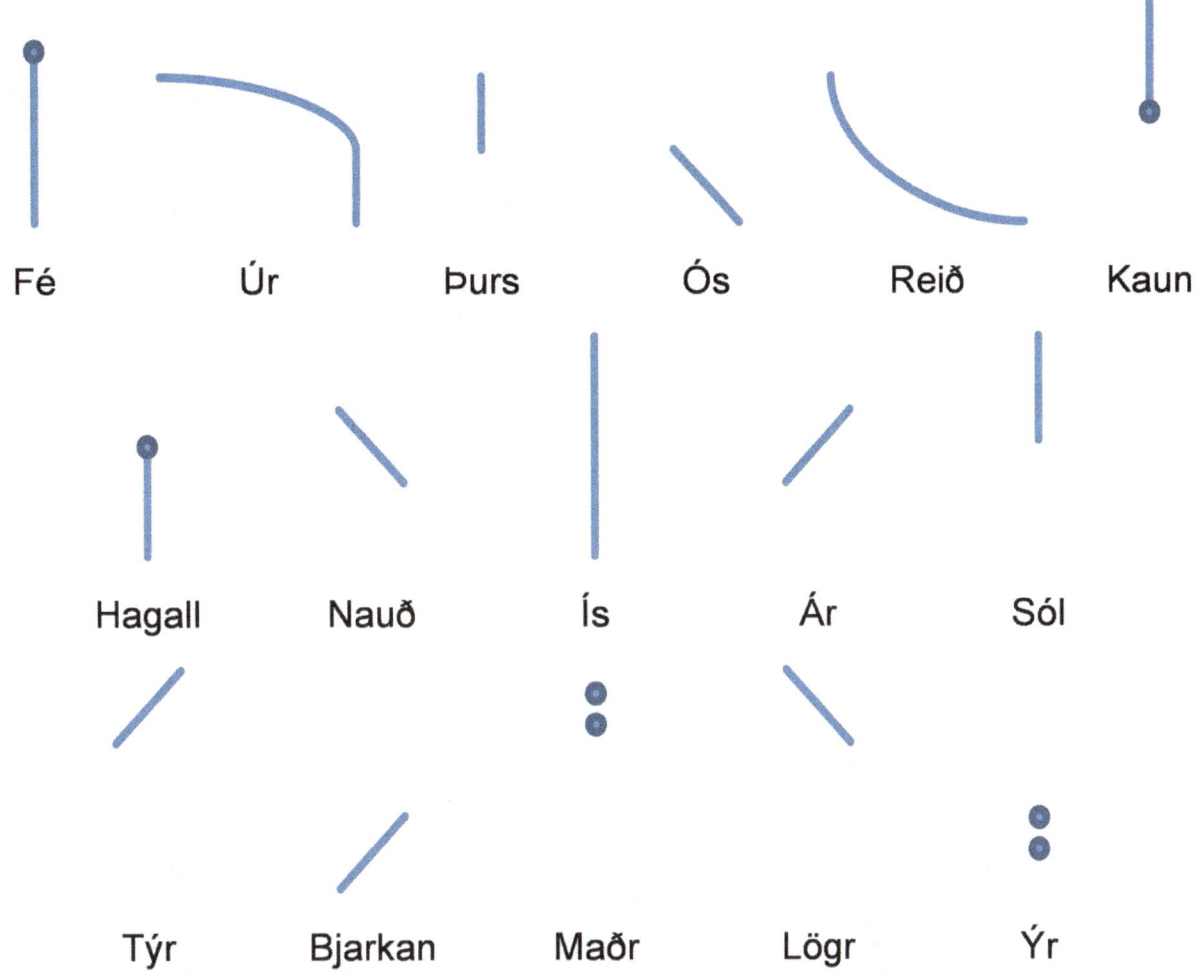

Hälsinge Staveless Runes are often thought to have functioned somewhat like a form of runic encryption. Their cryptic style may have been used to conceal messages, mark ownership discreetly, or serve as a kind of insider code within certain communities.

Encryption or shorthand helped prevent outsiders or enemies from easily reading sensitive information. Runes had strong associations with magic and ritual. Encrypted or cryptic runes might have been used to protect spells, charms, or curses, making their power 'hidden' from uninitiated eyes.

Secret or obscure runes could signify ownership, lineage, or social status, readable only by those 'in the know'. Viking Age societies had complex social hierarchies; encrypted runes might have served as a coded communication method within warrior bands or elite circles.

However, unlike deliberate ciphers, staveless runes seem more like a practical shorthand or stylistic variation that also had the side effect of being somewhat secretive.

1.9. Younger Fuþark (Orkney)

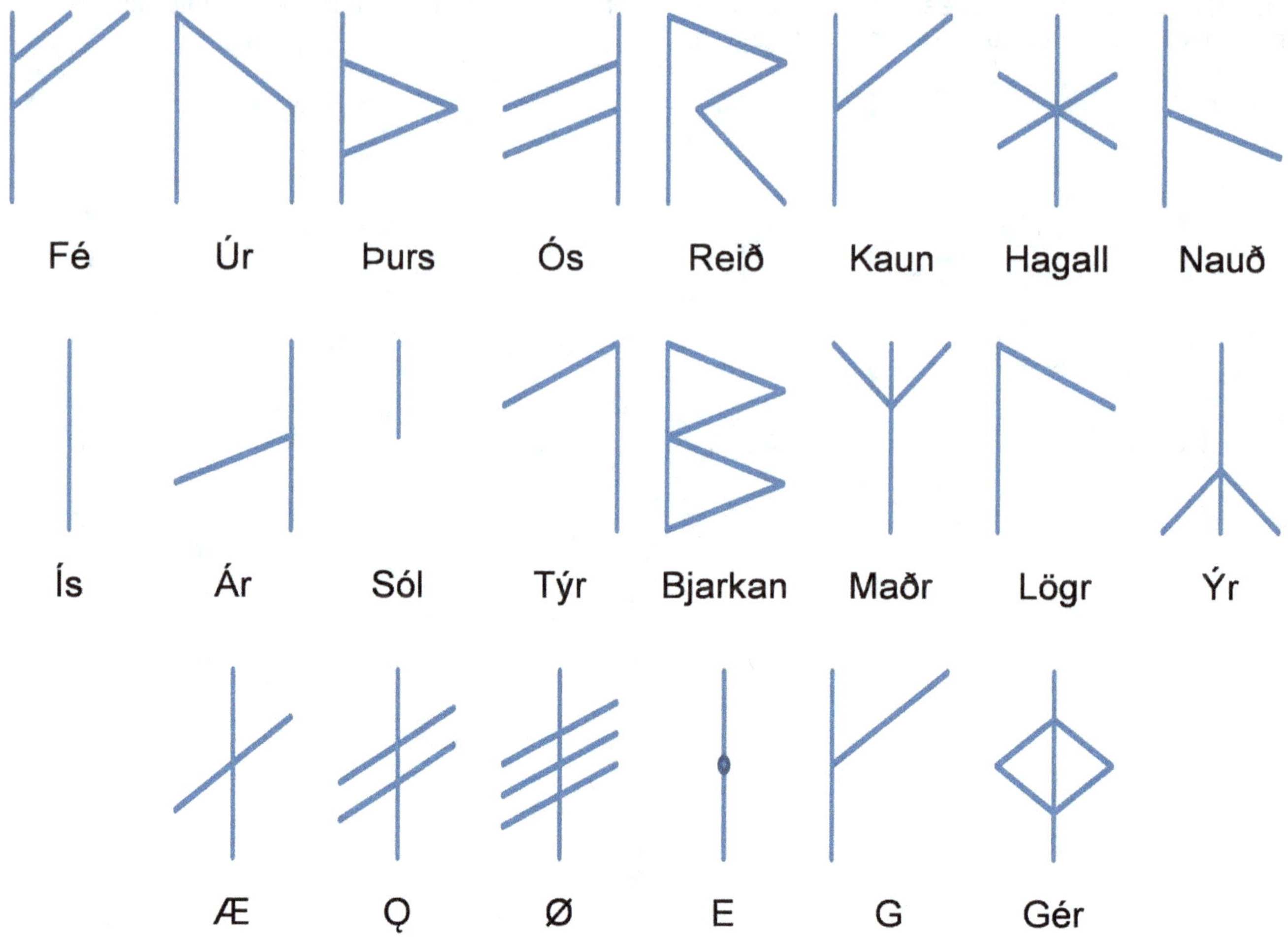

Fé	Úr	Þurs	Ós	Reið	Kaun	Hagall	Nauð
Ís	Ár	Sól	Týr	Bjarkan	Maðr	Lögr	Ýr
Æ	Ǫ	Ø	E	G	Gér		

Findings across the Northern Isles reveal a distinctive variation of the Younger Fuþark used by Norse settlers from the 8th century onward. Due to Orkney's remote location, these runes developed somewhat independently, preserving archaic features and adopting unique innovations not always seen in mainland Scandinavian inscriptions. While the first 16 runes closely match other Younger Fuþark variants, the addition of extra sounds shows that local evolution had already begun.

The style of Orkney runes reflects a blend of Scandinavian runic traditions with local artistic influences, likely shaped by stone-carving customs as well as Pictish and Celtic art. This fusion is evident in the distinctive letter shapes and carving techniques found in the region.

Unlike many runic inscriptions elsewhere that are purely pagan or secular, many Orkney rune stones integrate Christian iconography such as crosses alongside traditional runic text. This combination indicates the islands' gradual Christianisation while retaining elements of Norse cultural identity, creating a unique syncretic blend of belief systems.

The inscriptions often commemorate local individuals and reflect place names specific to Orkney, highlighting the region's distinct identity. Overall, Orkney runes exemplify the dynamic cultural exchange and adaptation occurring at the crossroads of Norse, Celtic, and Christian worlds during the Viking Age.

1.10. Younger Fuþark (Manx-Jeran)

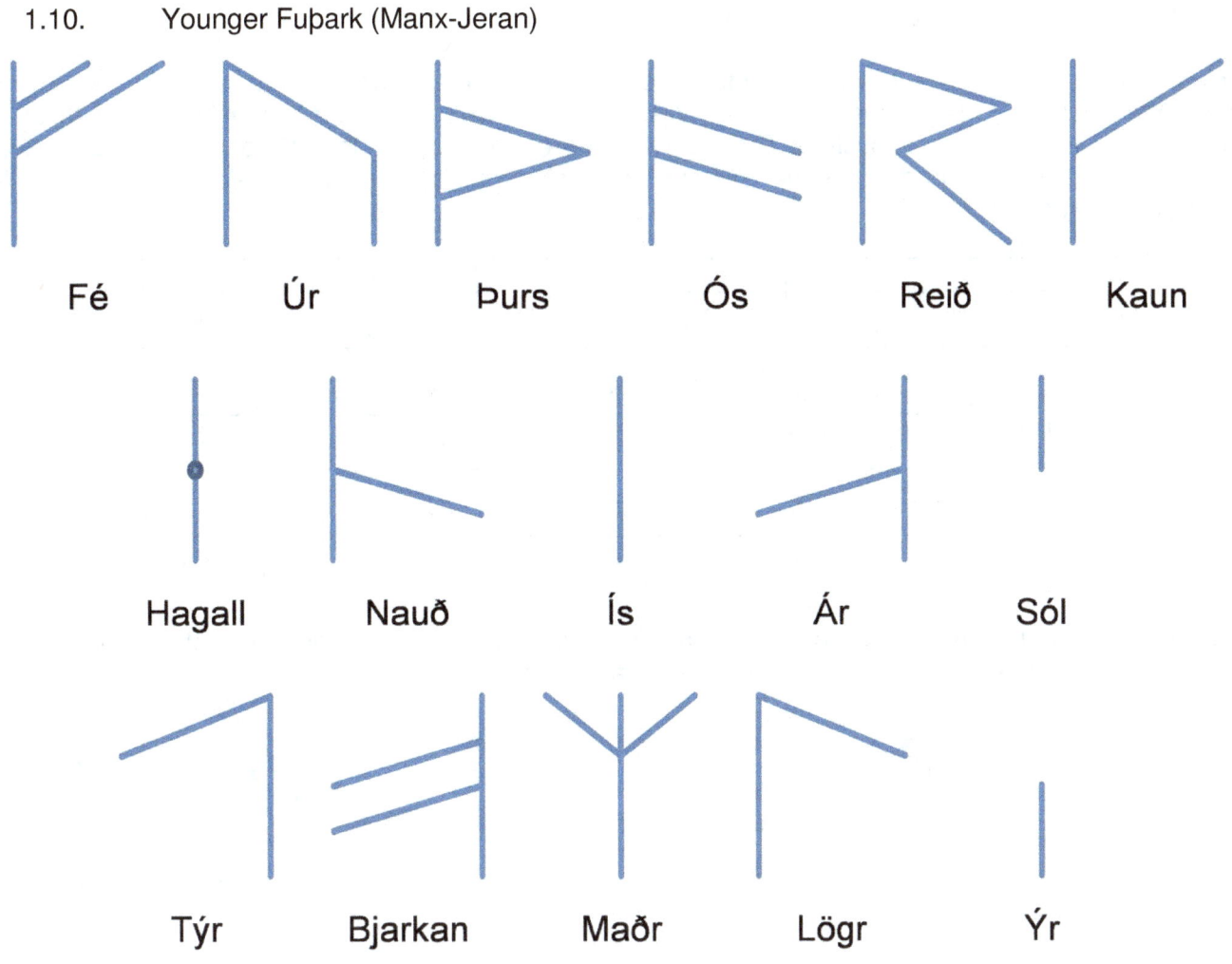

Manx-Jeran Runes were used primarily on the Isle of Man from around the 10th to 12th centuries. Like the Orkney runes, they show altered rune forms tailored to local Norse-Gaelic speech.

The Norse population of the Isle of Man left behind around 26 rune stones. Their visual style reflects a blend of Scandinavian and Celtic artistic motifs, such as knotwork and interlace, creating a hybrid aesthetic unique to the region. Pagan symbols and traditional runes appear alongside Christian imagery like crosses and invocations, revealing a society navigating the shift from Norse beliefs to Christianity without entirely discarding its spiritual roots.

Unlike the more standardized runic alphabets used in parts of Scandinavia, the Manx-Jeran runes were often informally hybridised, showing cross-cultural experimentation rather than strict adherence to a runic canon. In some cases, runes were used decoratively or symbolically rather than linguistically, further distancing them from the purely textual role seen in other regions, standing apart from more conservative Scandinavian runic traditions.

Some of the runes are consistent with the Short Twig variety, and the 'Bjarkan' rune appears to be a reversed version of the Short Twig version.

1.11. Younger Fuþark (Twig Runes)

Twig runes are a form of runic encryption that modifies the standard shapes of runes by breaking them down into systematic branches or 'twigs'. This made the writing appear unfamiliar and difficult to interpret without knowing the system. They are deciphered by counting the number of twigs on the left and the right. The left twig denotes the 'row', and the right twig denotes the 'character' in that row, like a 'locator' or 'address'.

1/1	1/2	1/3	1/4	1/5	1/6
ᚠ	ᚢ	ᚦ	ᚬ	ᚱ	ᚴ

2/1	2/2	2/3	2/4	2/5
ᚼ	ᚾ	ᛁ	ᛅ	ᛋ

3/1	3/2	3/3	3/4	3/5
ᛏ	ᛒ	ᛘ	ᛚ	ᛦ

The distinction between each word is made my changing whether the twigs (left, right, or both) stem from the top or the bottom. In this set, both the left and right twigs stem from the top:

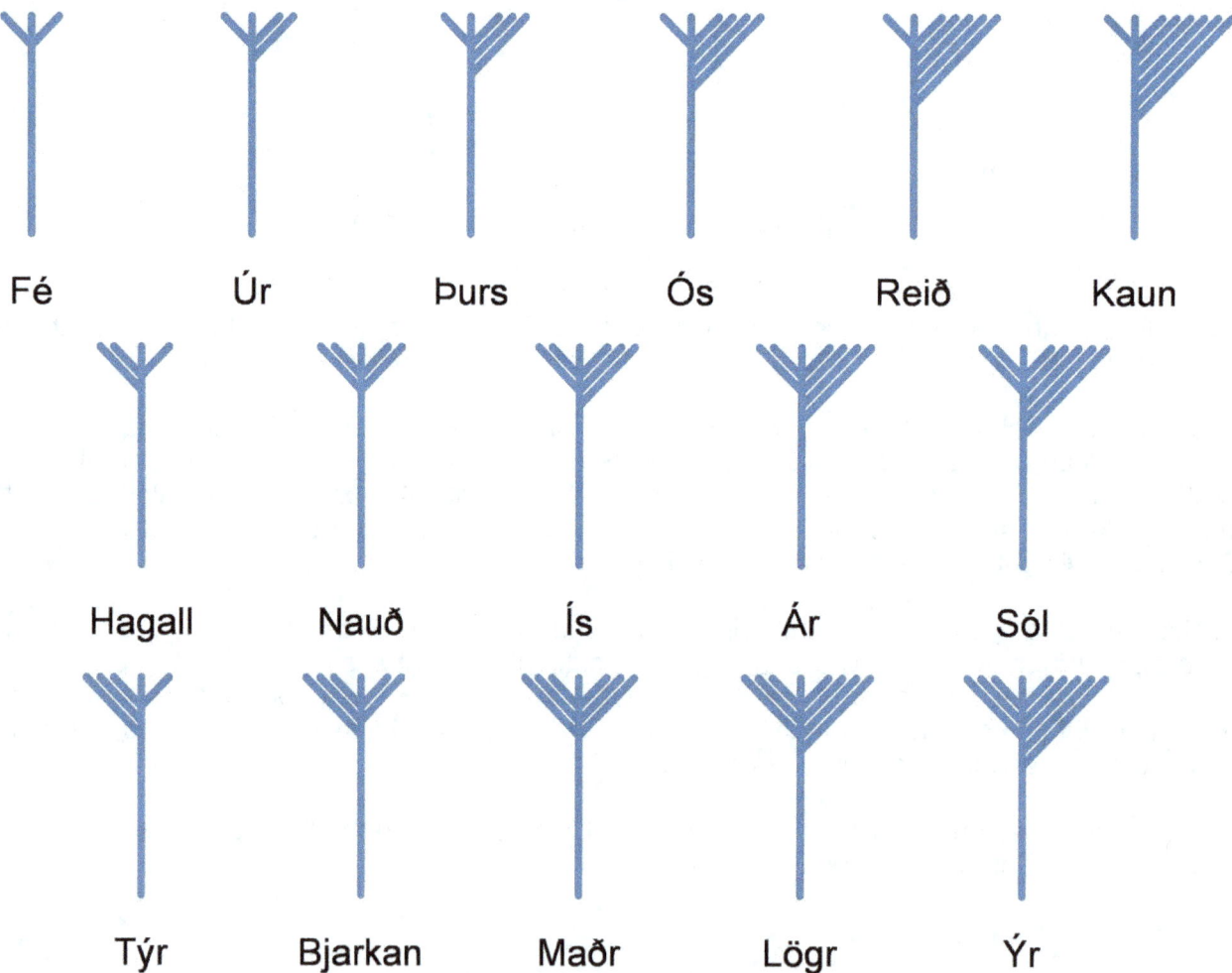

Fé   Úr   Þurs   Ós   Reið   Kaun

Hagall   Nauð   Ís   Ár   Sól

Týr   Bjarkan   Maðr   Lögr   Ýr

In this set, the left twigs stem from the bottom:

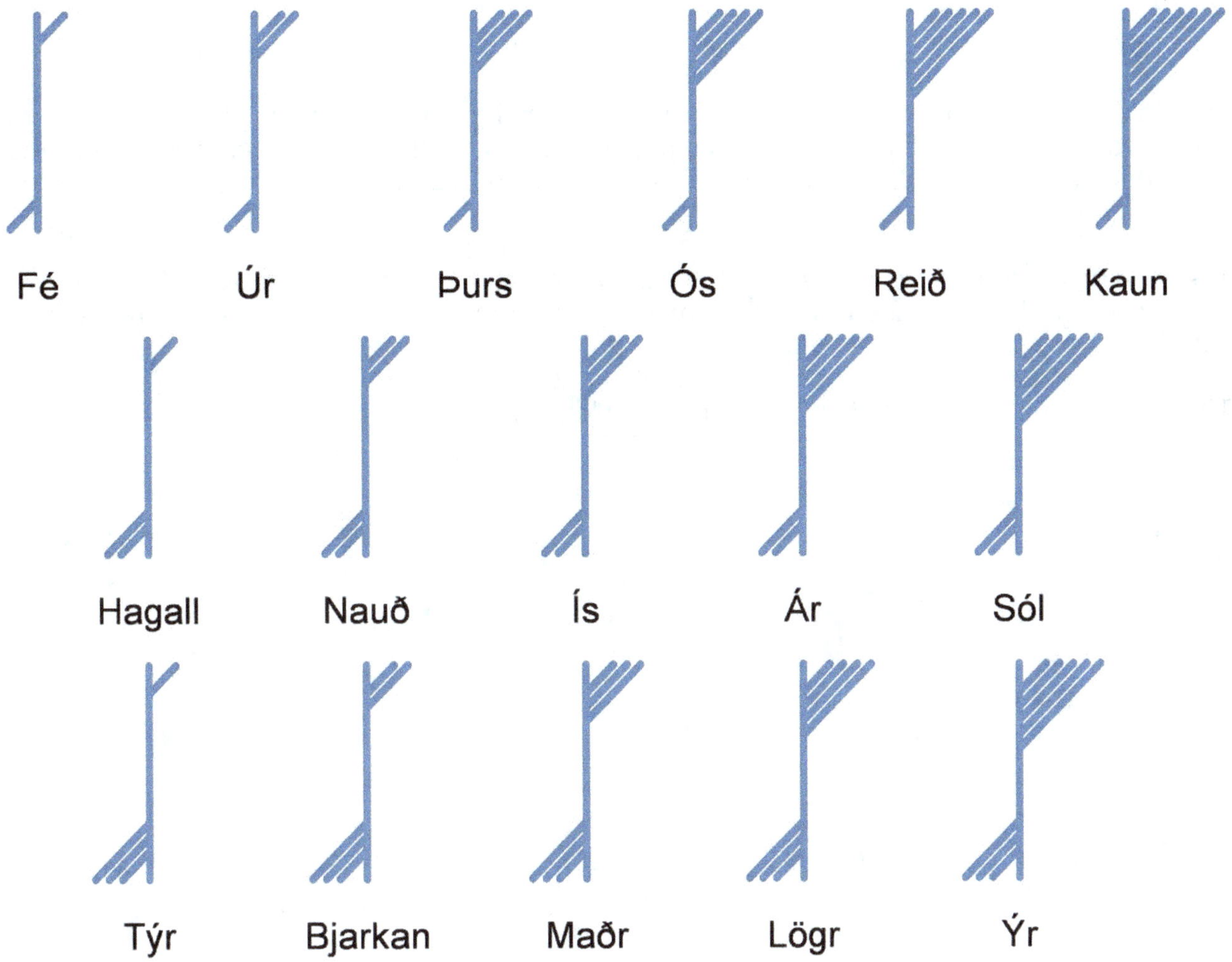

Fé Úr Þurs Óss Reið Kaun

Hagall Nauð Ís Ár Sól

Týr Bjarkan Maðr Lögr Ýr

Example Text (Ek hetr Mathias = I am called Matthew)

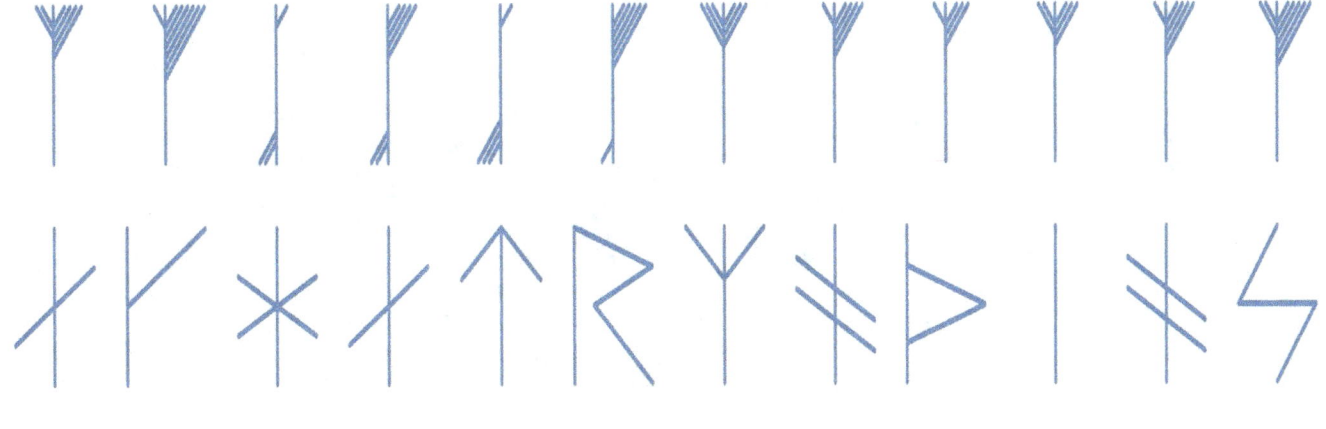

E K H E T R M A Þ I A S

1.12. Younger Fuþark (Tent Runes)

Tent runes are a later form of cryptography that takes the Twig Runes a step further by combining two Twig Runes together and overlapping them into one symbol representing two letters.

The Rök Runestone in Rök (Östergötland, Sweden) features several tent runes along the top row of its back face. Evidence for tent runes also comes from Icelandic manuscripts, especially from the 17th–18th centuries, like 'Runologia' by Jón Ólafsson, which describes how tent runes are constructed and used.

The advantage of this system is that with each tent rune containing two twig runes, the resulting encryption can be expressed in half as many characters, i.e. six tent runes can represent twelve letters.

The first letter uses a twig that slants from the top left to the borrom tight.

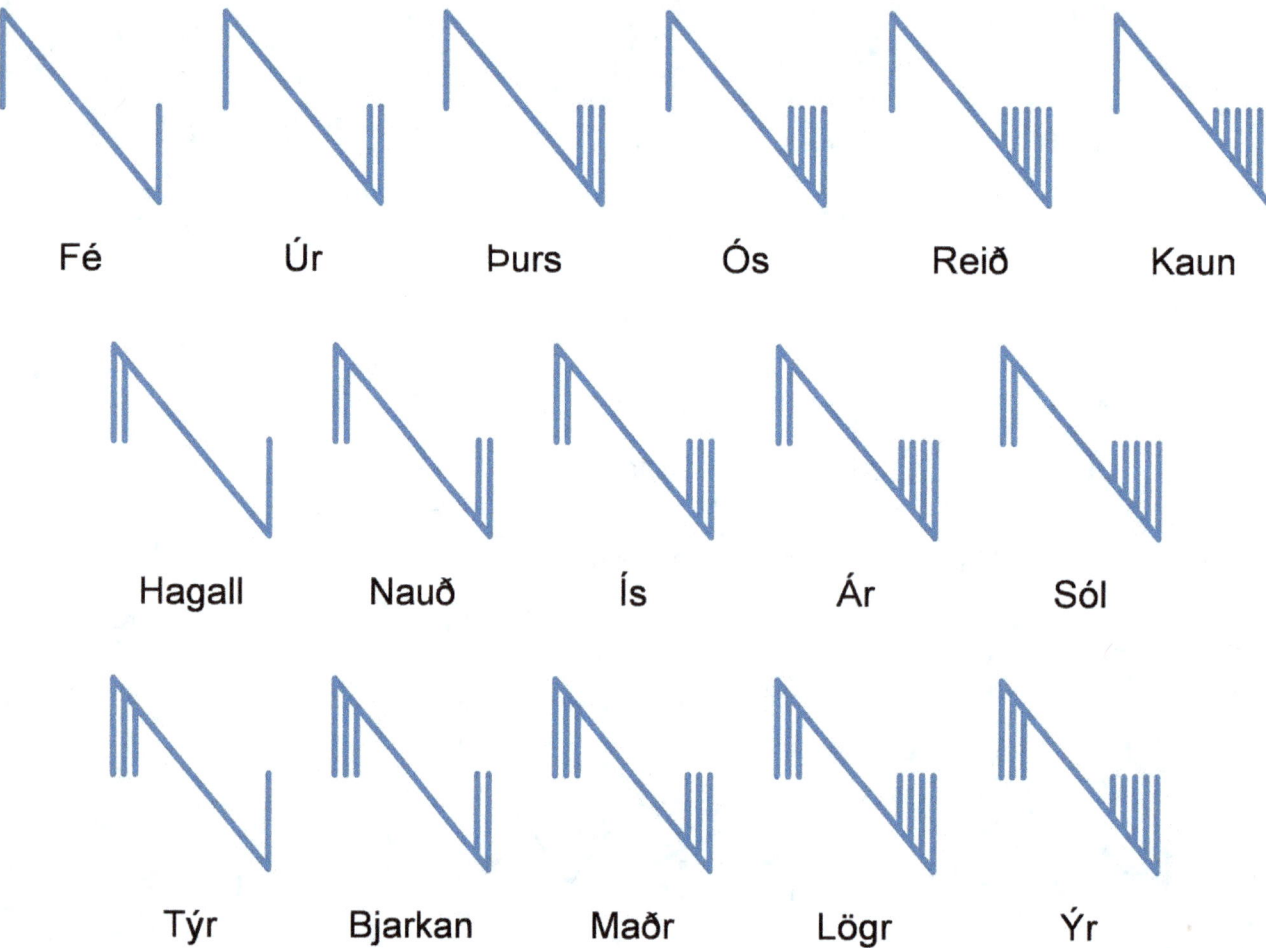

The second letter uses a twig that slants from the top right to the bottom left.

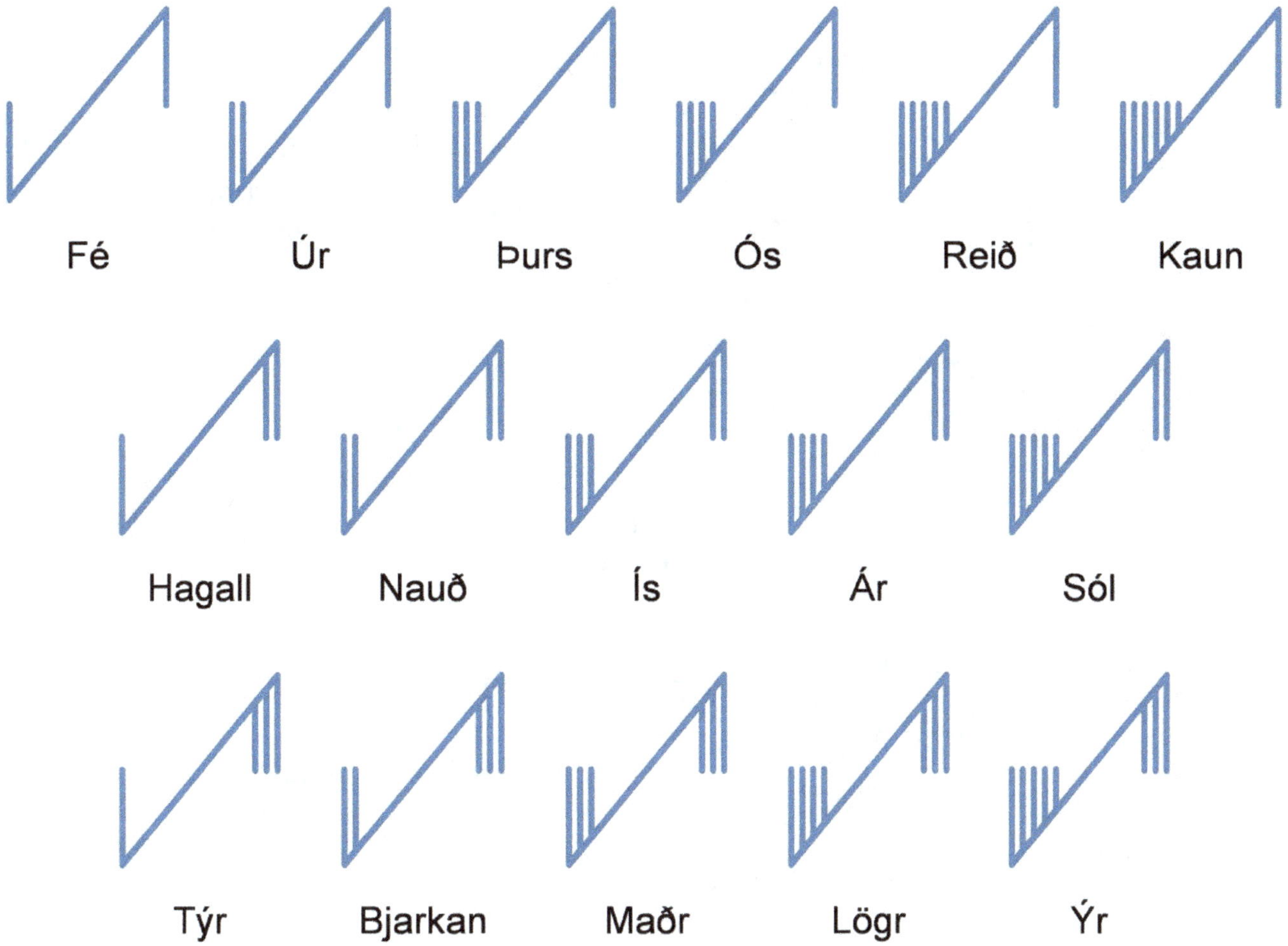

| Fé | Úr | Þurs | Ós | Reið | Kaun |

| Hagall | Nauð | Ís | Ár | Sól |

| Týr | Bjarkan | Maðr | Lögr | Ýr |

Example Text (Ek hetr Mathias = I am called Matthew)

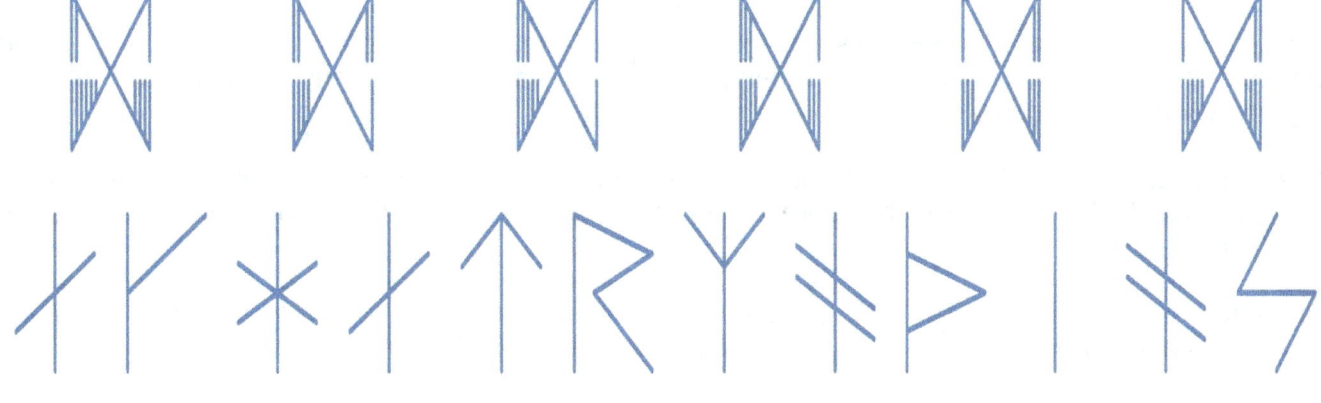

E K H E T R M A Þ I A S

1.13. Icelandic Fuþark

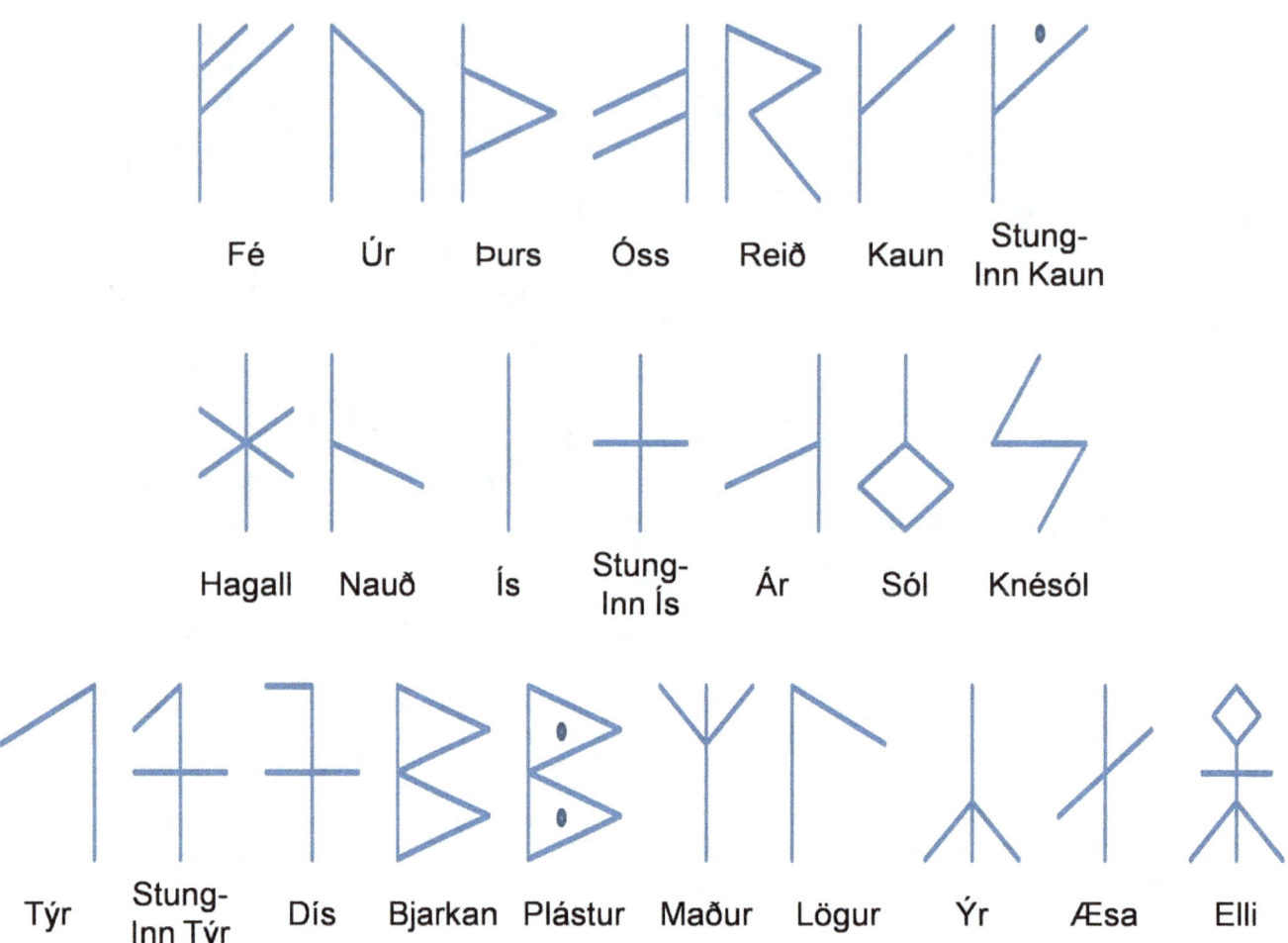

From the settlement of Iceland in the latter half of the 9th century, the Younger Fuþark that the settlers brought with them acquired additions slowly and steadily until around the 17th century to reflect new sounds or new uses of runes in favour of others that had fallen out of use.

There also exist several 'Rune Poems' which describe the meaning of each rune. These can be found in a number of different manuscripts all varying slightly from each other, perhaps because of evolution, regional variation, or scribal error.

The meanings given in the Icelandic Rune Poems appear to be much darker than its predecessors, perhaps to reflect the very tough nature of life that the people of Iceland faced in such a harsh landscape.

The latest edition of the rune 'Elli' is believed to have taken place around 1680 based on the manuscript containing the 'Later Icelandic Rune Poem' (78v, AM 738 4to).

1.14. Greenlandic Runes

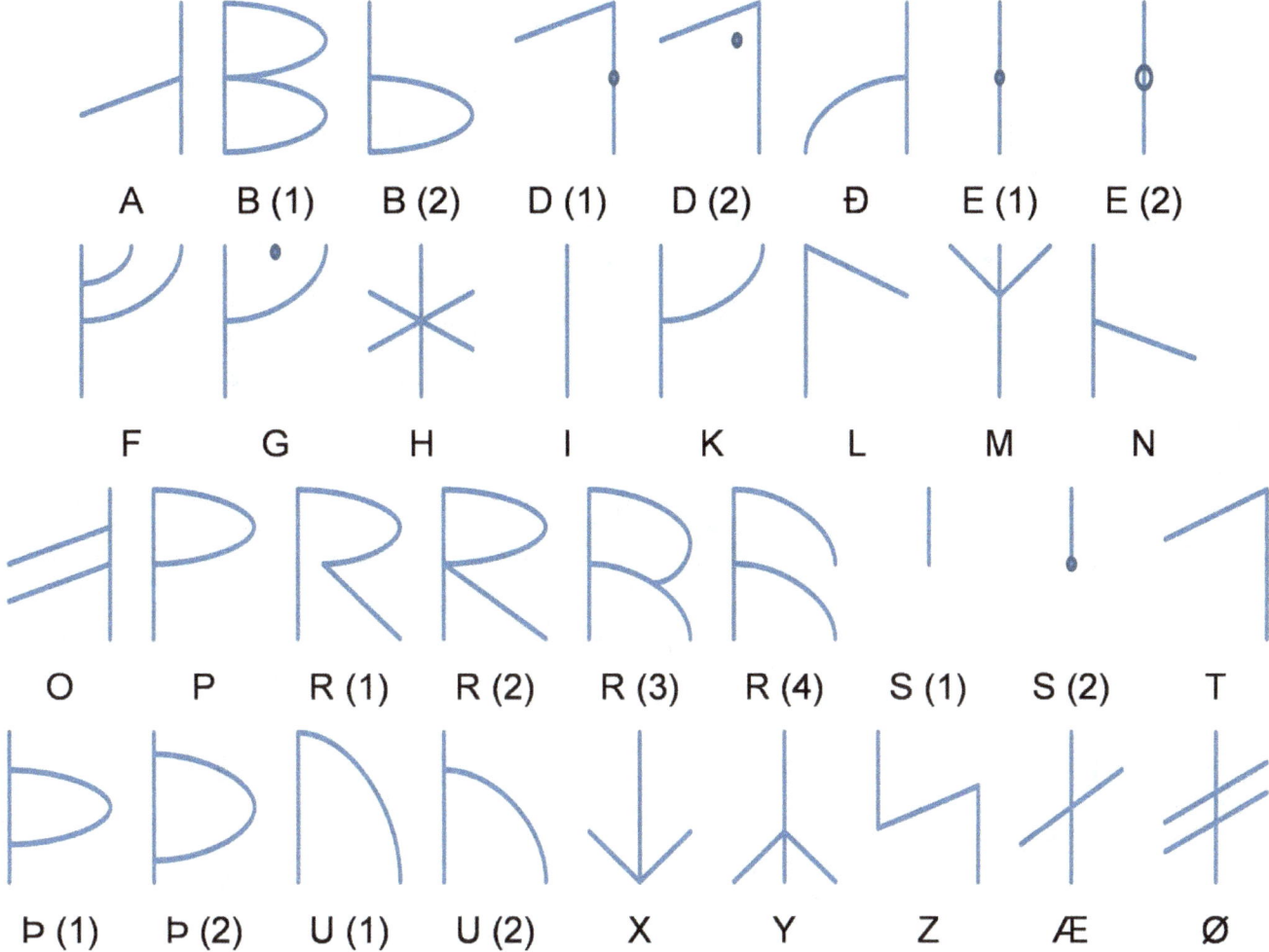

Norse settlers in Greenland from the 10th to 15th centuries used a localised form of the Younger Futhark. These runes reflect Old Norse gradually evolving into a distinct Old Greenlandic Norse, influenced by the region's isolation. Some inscriptions show orthographic variation, likely due to the colony's distance from mainland linguistic developments.

The most notable example is the Kingittorsuaq Runestone, found in 1824 on an island near Upernavik and dated to around 1300 CE. It commemorates the building of a stone cairn by three Norsemen and shows standard runes with minor local variations. Other inscriptions, mostly fragmentary, have been found at Brattahlíð (Erik the Red's estate) and several church sites in the Eastern Settlement.

Most Greenlandic runes reflect a Christianised Norse culture, especially from the 11th century onward. Inscriptions often include crosses or invocations to God, contrasting with the more pagan or magical tone of earlier Scandinavian rune use. These texts were typically memorial or practical in nature.

Runic literacy in Greenland may have lasted into the 15th century, well after it had faded in most of Scandinavia. This suggests Greenland was one of the final strongholds of traditional runic writing.

1.15. Medieval Runes

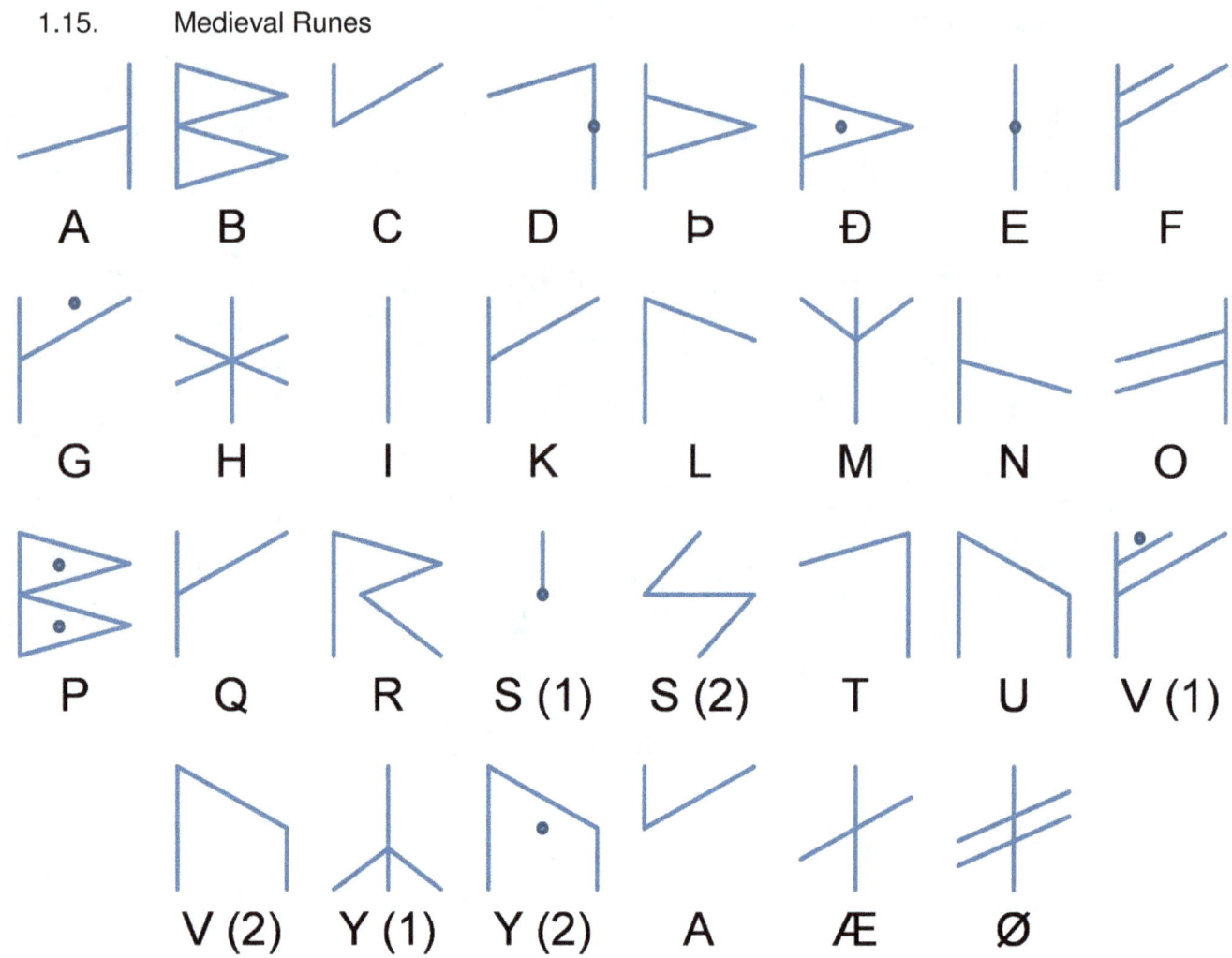

Between the 11th and 13th centuries, after the Viking Age, the runic writing system went through major changes. The original Younger Fuþark had only 16 runes, many of which stood for more than one sound. To make writing clearer and more accurate, new runes with small dots, called dotted runes, were added to show sound differences. This expanded the alphabet to about 27 runes, with each one representing a single sound.

At the same time, the Latin alphabet was becoming more popular in Scandinavia due to the spread of Christianity. Latin was used by the Church, in schools, and for legal documents, and it became a symbol of education and authority. In reaction to this, there was a brief revival of runes, possibly as a way to hold on to traditional culture.

A key example of this revival is the Codex Runicus, a 202-page manuscript written entirely in runes. It records the Scanian Laws and shows that runes were still seen as useful and important, even for serious legal writing.

However, some scholars believe this comeback of runes wasn't a step forward, but rather an effort to stop them from disappearing. Instead of showing progress, they see it as a sign that people were aware the runes were being replaced by Latin, and were trying to keep them alive for cultural or sentimental reasons.

1.16. Dalecarlian Runes

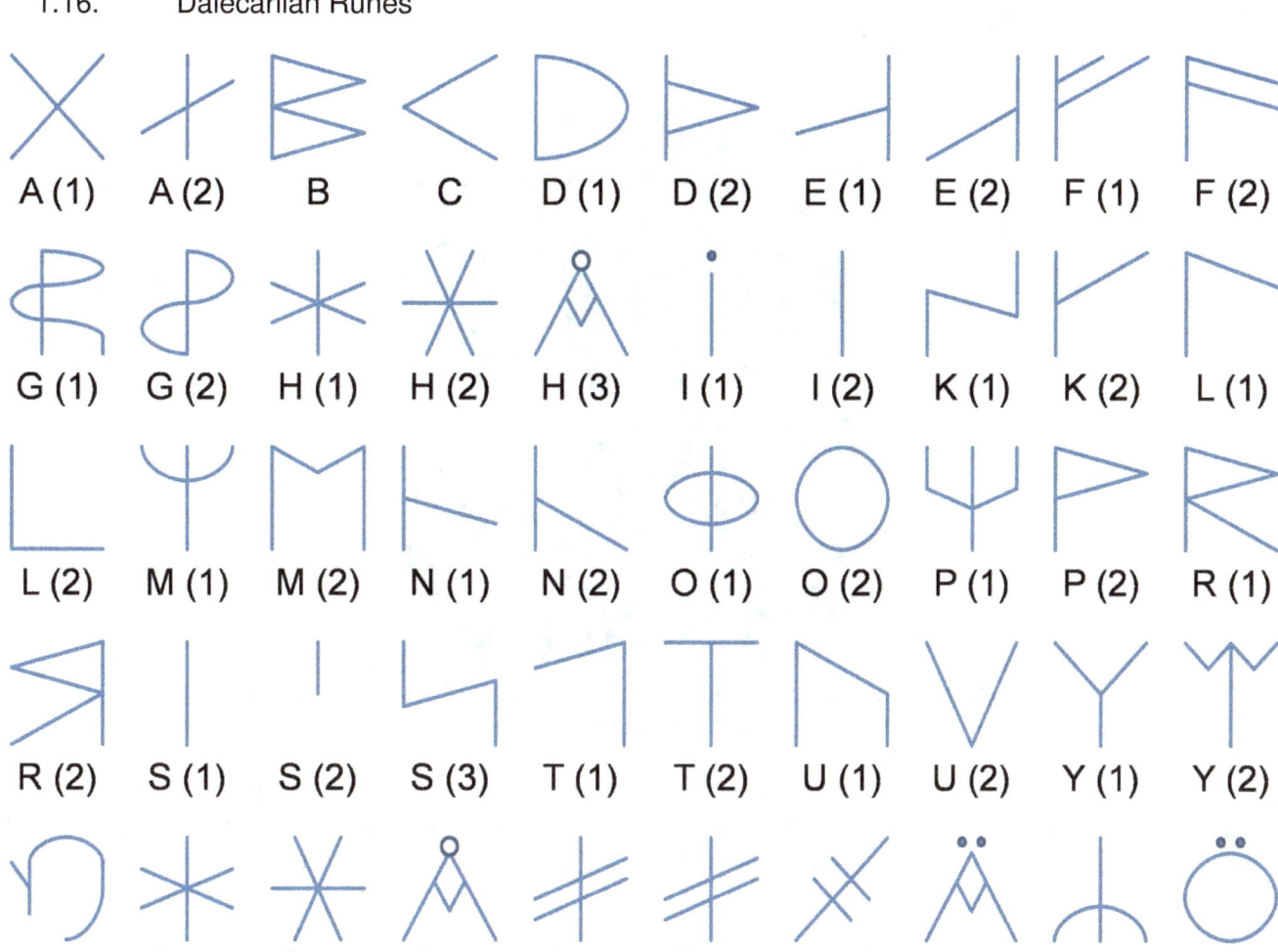

Dalecarlian runes, also known as Dalecarlian script or Elfdalian runes, are a unique and late form of the runic alphabet that survived in the Swedish province of Dalarna (especially in the area of Älvdalen) long after runes had fallen out of regular use elsewhere in Scandinavia.

They were in use from around the 16th century up until the early 20th century, which is remarkably late for any runic script. They existed alongside the Latin alphabet, and many inscriptions even mixed runic and Latin letters.

The script is a hybrid system, blending traditional runes with Latin letterforms. Over time, the runes were modified or replaced with Latin characters that resembled or replaced their phonetic function. This mix made the script look unique, partly medieval runes, partly handwritten Latin letters. The number and form of characters varied between villages and families, as there was no fixed standard.

Dalecarlian runes were mostly used for folk purposes: carving names, notes, or labels on tools, furniture, buildings, or even trees. They were not used for official documents or widespread communication, but rather for local, practical, or personal uses. Their survival was largely due to the isolation of Dalarna and strong local traditions.

They were often used to write Elfdalian (Älvdalska), a conservative North Germanic dialect with many archaic features. Elfdalian is still spoken by some in Älvdalen today and is undergoing revitalisation efforts. By the early 20th century, the use of Dalecarlian runes had mostly died out. Today, they are of interest mainly to historians, linguists, and enthusiasts of Nordic heritage.

2. Mythology

The Norns Urðr, Verðandi, and Skuld under Yggdrasil by Ludwig Burger, 1882
(Source: Wikipedia Creative Commons)

The runes were created by the Norns. The Norns are female beings that that live in a hall by the Well of Fate. The Norns throw lots, carve runes, water the world tree Yggdrasil to keep it healthy and green, and they weave the Web of Fate which decides the fates for all humans and gods alike. Their names are:

Urðr	past	'that which was'
Verðandi	being	'that which is becoming'
Skuld	necessity	'what will be'

There are two great houses of gods, the Æsir (Asgard) and the Vanir (Vanaheim). There was a great war between the two houses, which the Vanir won because of their ability to foretell the future.

After the war, there was peace and an exchange of gods to each of the houses. Njörðr, Frey, and Freyja went from Vanaheim to Asgard, and Hœnir went from Asgard to Vanaheim.

Odin vowed to himself to even the odds, and sacrificed himself to himself as the ruler of all the gods in order to gain knowledge and mastery of the runes. He pierced himself with a spear and hung himself upside down from the branches of Yggdrasil the world tree for 9 days, gazing into the Well of Fate. He also persuaded Freyja to teach him skills in magic.

Runes   *2. Mythology*

The Web of Urðr

The Web of Urðr (also known in Anglo-Saxon as 'Wyrd') is the common name for a powerful symbol out of which all runes can be found. It contains 9 interlocking lines, representing the 9 worlds, but also representing the web itself, out of which all things (in this case runes) are made possible.

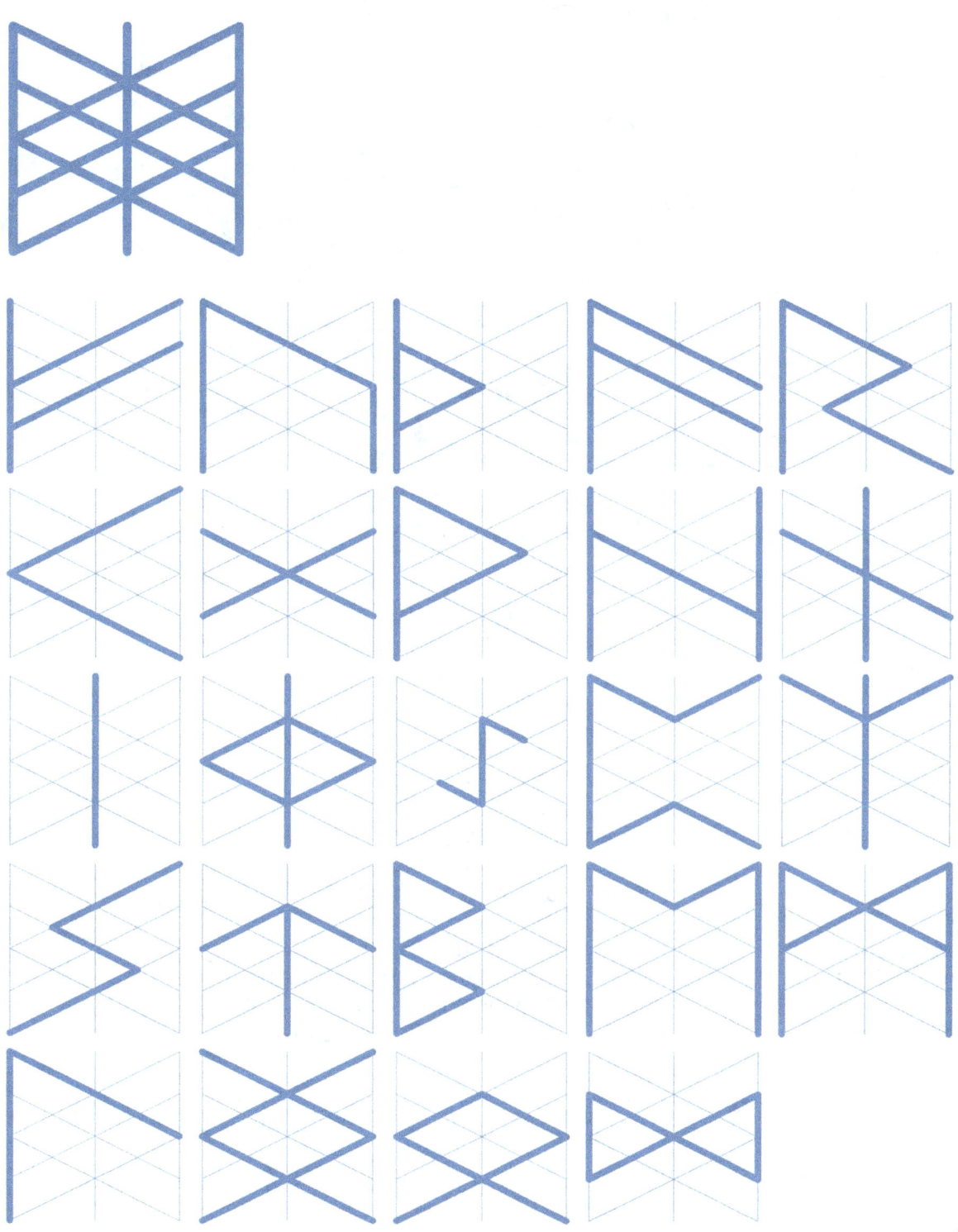

25

Völuspá

A Völva tells Odin about the creation of the world, and her prophecy of the end of the world in Ragnarök.

Odin and the Völva (Lorenz Frølich, 1895)
(Source: Wikipedia Creative Commons)

20. Þaðan koma meyjar
margs vitandi
þrjár ór þeim sæ,
er und þolli stendr;
Urð hétu eina,
aðra Verðandi,
- skáru á skíði, -
Skuld ina þriðju;
þær lög lögðu,
þær líf kuru
alda börnum,
örlög seggja.

20. Thence come maidens,
much knowing,
three from the hall,
which under that tree stands
Urd is called the one,
the second Verdandi,
on a tablet they graved—
Skuld the third.
Laws they established,
life allotted
to the sons of men;
destinies pronounced.

60. Finnask æsir á Iðavelli
ok um moldþinur máttkan dæma
ok minnask þar á megindóma
ok á Fimbultýs fornar rúnir.

60. The gods in Ithavoll meet together,
Of the terrible girdler of earth they talk,
And the mighty past they call to mind,
And the ancient runes of the Ruler of Gods.

Hávamál

A poem of the Odin's advice and philosophy, containing the Rúnatal, an account of how Odin sacrificed himself to gain knowledge and mastery of the runes.

Odin sacrificing himself upon Yggdrasil (Lorenz Frølich, 1895)
(Source: Wikipedia Creative Commons)

80. Þat er þá reynt,
er þú að rúnum spyrr
inum reginkunnum,
þeim er gerðu ginnregin
ok fáði fimbulþulr,
þá hefir hann bazt, ef hann þegir.

111. Mál er at þylja
þular stóli á
Urðarbrunni at,
sá ek ok þagðak,
sá ek ok hugðak,
hlýdda ek á manna mál;
of rúnar heyrða ek dæma,
né of ráðum þögðu
Háva höllu at,

80. That is now proved,
what you asked of the runes,
of the potent famous ones,
which the great gods made,
and the mighty sage stained,
that it is best for him if he stays silent.

111. I heard discourse,
From the seat of the sage,
Of things divine,
I also saw silence,
I also saw thought,
I heard the speech of men;
too runes I heard discussed,
nor overly silent
at the High One's hall.

Runes   *2. Mythology*

Háva höllu í,
heyrða ek segja svá:

In the High One's hall.
I hear say this:

138. Veit ec at ec hecc vindga meiði a
netr allar nío,
geiri vndaþr oc gefinn Oðin,
sialfr sialfom mer,
a þeim meiþi, er mangi veit, hvers hann af rótom renn.

138. I know that I hung on a windy tree
nine long nights,
wounded with a spear, dedicated to Odin,
myself to myself,
on that tree of which no man knows from where its roots run.

139. Við hleifi mic seldo ne viþ hornigi,
nysta ec niþr,
nam ec vp rvnar,
opandi nam,
fell ec aptr þaðan.

139. No bread did they give me nor a drink from a horn,
downwards I peered;
I took up the runes,
screaming I took them,
then I fell back from there.

142. Rúnar munt þú finna
ok ráðna stafi,
mjök stóra stafi,
mjök stinna stafi,
er fáði fimbulþulr
ok gerðu ginnregin
ok reist hroftr rögna.

142. Runes you must find,
And the meaningful symbols,
Very great symbols,
Very strong symbols,
Which the mighty sage stained
And the great powers made
And cut from among the powers

Sigrdrífumál

The Valkyrie Brynhild teaches Sigurd about the use of runic magic.

The Ramsund Carving, Sweden, 11th Century
(Source: Wikipedia Creative Commons)

05. Biór fori ec þer brynþings apaldr!
magni blandinn oc megintíri;
fullr er hann lioþa oc licnstafa,
godra galdra oc gamanruna.

05. Beer I bring thee, tree of battle,
Mingled of strength and mighty fame;
Charms it holds and healing signs,
Spells full good, and gladness-runes.

06. Sigrúnar þú skalt kunna,
ef þú vilt sigr hafa,
ok rísta á hialti hiǫrs,
sumar á véttrimum,
sumar á valbǫstum,
ok nefna tysvar Tý

06. Victory runes you must know
if you will have victory,
and carve them on the sword's hilt,
some on the grasp
and some on the inlay,
and name Tyr twice.

07. Ölrúnar skaltu kunna,
ef þú vill annars kvæn
véli-t þik í tryggð, ef þú trúir;
á horni skal þær rísta
ok á handar baki
ok merkja á nagli Nauð.

07. Ale-runes learn,
that with lies the wife
Of another betray not thy trust;
On the horn thou shalt write,
and the backs of thy hands,
And Need shalt mark on thy nails.

08. Full skal signa
ok við fári sjá
ok verpa lauki í lög;
þá ek þat veit,
at þér verðr aldri
meinblandinn mjöðr.

08. Thou shalt bless the draught,
and danger escape,
And cast a leek in the cup;
(For so I know
thou never shalt see
Thy mead with evil mixed.)

09. Bjargrúnar skaltu kunna,
ef þú bjarga vilt
ok leysa kind frá konum;
á lófum þær skal rísta
ok of liðu spenna
ok biðja þá dísir duga.

10. Brimrúnar skaltu rísta,
ef þú vilt borgit hafa
á sundi seglmörum;
á stafni skal rísta
ok á stjórnarblaði
ok leggja eld í ár,
er-a svá brattr breki
né svá bláar unnir,
þó kemstu heill af hafi.

11. Limrúnar skaltu kunna,
af þú vilt læknir vera,
ok kunna sár at sjá;
á berki skal þær rísta
ok á baðmi viðar,
þeim er lúta austr limar.

12. Málrúnar skaltu kunna,
ef þú vilt, at manngi þér
heiftum gjaldi harm:
þær of vindr,
þær of vefr,
þær of setr allar saman
á því þingi,
er þjóðir skulu
í fulla dóma fara.

13. Hugrúnar skaltu kunna,
ef þú vilt hverjum vera
geðsvinnari guma;
þær of réð,
þær of reist,
þær of hugði Hroftr
af þeim legi,
er lekit hafði
ór hausi Heiðdraupnis
ok ór horni Hoddrofnis.

09. Birth-runes learn,
if help thou wilt lend,
The babe from the mother to bring;
On thy palms shalt write them,
and round thy joints,
And ask the fates to aid.

10. Wave-runes learn,
if well thou wouldst shelter
The sail-steeds out on the sea;
On the stem shalt thou write,
and the steering blade,
And burn them into the oars;
Though high be the breakers,
and black the waves,
Thou shalt safe the harbor seek.

11. Branch-runes learn,
if a healer wouldst be,
And cure for wounds wouldst work;
On the bark shalt thou write,
and on trees that be
With boughs to the eastward bent.

12. Speech-runes learn,
that none may seek
To answer harm with hate;
Well he winds
and weaves them all,
And sets them side by side,
At the judgment-place,
when justice there
The folk shall fairly win.

13. Thought-runes shall you learn,
If you wish to be who you are
Keenest of mind;
and them he wrote,
and then he made,
and them thought, Hroftr
Out of the draught
that down had dropped
From the head of Heithdraupnir,
And the horn of Hoddrofnir.

19. Þat eru bókrúnar,
þat eru bjargrúnar
ok allar ölrúnar
ok mætar meginrúnar,
hveim er þær kná óvilltar
ok óspilltar
sér at heillum hafa;
njóttu, ef þú namst,
unz rjúfask regin.

19. Beech-runes are there,
birth-runes are there,
And all the runes of ale,
And the magic runes of might;
Who knows them rightly
and reads them true,
Has them himself to help;
Ever they aid,
Till the gods are gone.

3. Meanings

The meanings for the Elder Fuþark and the Anglo-Saxon Fuþorc are based on the Anglo Saxon Rune Poem believed to have been composed in the 7th or 8th century. The original manuscript (Cotton Otho B.x) was copied in 1705 by George Hicks before it was destroyed in a fire in 1731.

The Anglo-Saxon Rune Poem as it appears in 'Linguarum Veterum Septentrionalium Thesaurus Grammatico-Criticus Et Archæologicus' by George Hicks, 1705
(Source: Wikipedia Creative Commons)

The meanings for the Younger Fuþark are based on the Icelandic Rune Poem (AM 687d 4° and AM 461 12°)

The meanings for the Icelandic Fuþark are based on the Late Icelandic Rune Poem (78v, AM 738 4to, c1680)

The Elder Fuþark and the Anglo-Saxon Rune Poem

No.	Rune	Name	Sound	Rune Poem	Translation	Divination Meanings
1	ᚠ	Fehu	/F/	Feoh byþ frofur fira gehwylcum; sceal ðeah manna gehwylc miclun hyt dælan gif he wile for drihtne domes hleotan.	Wealth is a comfort to all men; yet must every man bestow it freely, if he wish to gain honour in the sight of the Lord.	Profit, Prosperity, Money, Power, Wealth, Luck, Success, Happiness
2	ᚢ	Ūruz	/U(:)/	Ur byþ anmod ond oferhyrned, felafrecne deor, feohteþ mid hornum mære morstapa; þæt is modig wuht.	The aurochs is proud and has great horns; it is a very savage beast and fights with its horns; a great ranger of the moors, it is a creature of mettle.	Strength, Energy, Stamina, Will, Strength, Speed, Desire, Gateway
3	ᚦ	Thurisaz	/Θ/, /Ð/	Ðorn byþ ðearle scearp; ðegna gehwylcum anfeng ys yfyl, ungemetum reþe manna gehwelcum, ðe him mid resteð.	The thorn is exceedingly sharp, an evil thing for any knight to touch, uncommonly severe on all who sit among them.	Pain, Hindrance, Difficulties, Discipline, Meditation, Study
4	ᚨ	Ansuz	/A(:)/	Os byþ ordfruma ælere spræce, wisdomes wraþu ond witena frofur and eorla gehwam eadnys ond tohiht.	The mouth is the source of all language, a pillar of wisdom and a comfort to wise men, a blessing and a joy to every knight.	Speech, Wisdom, Source, Connection, Communication, Mouth

No.	Rune	Name	Sound	Rune Poem	Translation	Divination Meanings
5	ᚱ	Raidō	/R/	Rad byþ on recyde rinca gehwylcum sefte ond swiþhwæt, ðamðe sitteþ on ufan meare mægenheardum ofer milpaþas.	Riding seems easy to every warrior while he is indoors and very courageous to him who traverses the high-roads on the back of a stout horse.	Journey, Movement, Change, Orientation, Travel, Relocation, Dance of Life
6	ᚲ	Kenaz / Kaunan	/K/	Cen byþ cwicera gehwam, cuþ on fyre blac ond beorhtlic, byrneþ oftust ðær hi æþelingas inne restaþ.	The torch is known to every living man by its pale, bright flame; it always burns where princes sit within.	Fire, Wisdom, Enlightenment, Pain, Torch, Wisdom, Creativity
7	ᚷ	Gebō	/g/	Gyfu gumena byþ gleng and herenys, wraþu and wyrþscype and wræcna gehwam ar and ætwist, ðe byþ oþra leas.	Generosity brings credit and honour, which support one's dignity; it furnishes help and subsistence to all broken men who are devoid of aught else.	Generosity, Friendship, Hospitality, Honour, Gifts, Relationship
8	ᚹ	Wunjō	/W/	Wenne bruceþ, ðe can weana lyt sares and sorge and him sylfa hæfþ blæd and blysse and eac byrga geniht.	Bliss he enjoys who knows not suffering, sorrow nor anxiety, and has prosperity and happiness and a good enough house.	Happiness, Bliss, Love, Hope, Joy, Pleasure, Fellowship, Glory
9	ᚺ	Hagalaz	/H/	Hægl byþ hwitust corna; hwyrft hit of heofones lyfte, wealcaþ hit windes scura; weorþeþ hit to wætere syððan.	Hail is the whitest of grain; it is whirled from the vault of heaven and is tossed about by gusts of wind and then it melts into water.	Sudden Difficulties, Pain, Fortification, Hail, Drastic Change, Life Lessons

No.	Rune	Name	Sound	Rune Poem	Translation	Divination Meanings
10	ᚾ	Nauthiz / Naudiz	/N/	Nyd byþ nearu on breostan; weorþeþ hi þeah oft niþa bearnum to helpe and to hæle gehwæþre, gif hi his hlystaþ æror.	Trouble is oppressive to the heart; yet often it proves a source of help and salvation to the children of men, to everyone who heeds it betimes.	Trouble, Duress, Constraints, Necessity, Endurance, Survival, Determination, Patience
11	ᛁ	Isa / Īsaz	/I(:)/	Is byþ ofereald, ungemetum slidor, glisnaþ glæshluttur gimmum gelicust, flor forste geworuht, fæger ansyne.	Ice is very cold and immeasurably slippery; it glistens as clear as glass and most like to gems; it is a floor wrought by the frost, fair to look upon.	Cold, Hindrance, Immobility, Bridge, Challenge, reinforcement, Standoff
12	ᛄ	Jēra	/J/	Ger byþ gumena hiht, ðonne God læteþ, halig heofones cyning, hrusan syllan beorhte bleda beornum ond ðearfum.	Summer is a joy to men, when God, the holy King of Heaven, suffers the earth to bring forth shining fruits for rich and poor alike.	Year, Earth, Harvest, Livelihood, Year, Change, Cycle, Reward
13	ᛇ	Īhwaz / Eihwaz	/Æ:/(?)	Eoh byþ utan unsmeþe treow, heard hrusan fæst, hyrde fyres, wyrtrumun underwreþyd, wyn on eþle.	The yew is a tree with rough bark, hard and fast in the earth, supported by its roots, a guardian of flame and a joy upon an estate.	Endurance, Strength, Death, Creation, Transformation, Turning Point, Yew
14	ᛈ	Perthro / Perth	/P/	Peorð byþ symble plega and hlehter wlancum [on middum], ðar wigan sittaþ on beorsele bliþe ætsomne.	Peorth is a source of recreation and amusement to the great, where warriors sit blithely together in the banqueting-hall.	Joy, Feasting, Drinking Parties, Celebration, Mysteries, Secrets, Occult Abilities

No.	Rune	Name	Sound	Rune Poem	Translation	Divination Meanings
15	ᛉ	Algiz	/Z/	Eolh-secg eard hæfþ oftust on fenne wexeð on wature, wundaþ grimme, blode breneð beorna gehwylcne ðe him ænigne onfeng gedeþ.	The Eolh-sedge is mostly to be found in a marsh; it grows in the water and makes a ghastly wound, covering with blood every warrior who touches it.	Death, Life, Protection, Protection, Support, Sanctuary
16	ᛋ	Sōwilō	/S/	Sigel semannum symble biþ on hihte, ðonne hi hine feriaþ ofer fisces beþ, oþ hi brimhengest bringeþ to lande.	The sun is ever a joy in the hopes of seafarers when they journey away over the fishes' bath, until the courser of the deep bears them to land.	Guiding Light, Anchor, Life, Clockwork, Sun, Health, Energy, Power
17	ᛏ	Tīwaz / Teiwaz	/T/	Tir biþ tacna sum, healdeð trywa wel wiþ æþelingas; a biþ on færylde ofer nihta genipu, næfre swiceþ.	Tiw is a guiding star; well does it keep faith with princes; it is ever on its course over the mists of night and never fails.	Victory, Battle, Omen, Guide, Justice, Authority, Analysis, Rationslity
18	ᛒ	Berkano / Berkanan	/B/	Beorc byþ bleda leas, bereþ efne swa ðeah tanas butan tudder, biþ on telgum wlitig, heah on helme hrysted fægere, geloden leafum, lyfte getenge.	The poplar bears no fruit; yet without seed it brings forth suckers, for it is generated from its leaves. Splendid are its branches and gloriously adorned its lofty crown which reaches to the skies.	Light, Renewal, Femininity, Fertilisation, Birth, Fertility, Growth, Liberation, Love Affair

Runes — 3. Meanings

No.	Rune	Name	Sound	Rune Poem	Translation	Divination Meanings
19	ᛖ	Ehwaz	/E(:)/	Eh byþ for eorlum æþelinga wyn, hors hofum wlanc, ðær him hæleþ ymb[e] welege on wicgum wrixlaþ spræce and biþ unstyllum æfre frofur.	The horse is a joy to princes in the presence of warriors. A steed in the pride of its hoofs, when rich men on horseback bandy words about it; and it is ever a source of comfort to the restless.	Motion, Reliability, Connection, Destiny, Movement, Change, Harmony, Teamwork
20	ᛗ	Mannaz	/M/	Man byþ on myrgþe his magan leof: sceal þeah anra gehwylc oðrum swican, forðum drihten wyle dome sine þæt earme flæsc eorþan betæcan.	The joyous man is dear to his kinsmen; yet every man is doomed to fail his fellow, since the Lord by his decree will commit the vile carrion to the earth.	Mankind, Faithfulness, Companionship, Friendship, Self, Human Race, Social Order, Awareness
21	ᛚ	Laguz	/L/	Lagu byþ leodum langsum geþuht, gif hi sculun neþan on nacan tealtum and hi sæyþa swyþe bregaþ and se brimhengest bridles ne gym[eð].	The ocean seems interminable to men, if they venture on the rolling bark and the waves of the sea terrify them and the courser of the deep heed not its bridle.	Mutability, Flow, Mystery, Water, Life Energy, Imagination, Dreams
22	ᛜ / ᛝ	Ingwaz	/ŋ/	Ing wæs ærest mid East-Denum gesewen secgun, oþ he siððan est ofer wæg gewat; wæn æfter ran; ðus Heardingas ðone hæle nemdun.	Ing was first seen by men among the East-Danes, till, followed by his chariot, he departed eastwards over the waves. So the Heardingas named the hero.	Forefather, Manhood, Seed, Consecration, Fertility, New Life, Completion

No.	Rune	Name	Sound	Rune Poem	Translation	Divination Meanings
23	ᛟ	Ōthila / Ōthala	/O(:)/	Eþel byþ oferleof æghwylcum men, gif he mot ðær rihtes and gerysena on brucan on bolde bleadum oftast.	An estate is very dear to every man, if he can enjoy there in his house whatever is right and proper in constant prosperity.	Family, Offspring, Home, Shelter, Heritage, Heirlooms, Land of Birth
24	ᛞ	Dagaz	/D/	Dæg byþ drihtnes sond, deore mannum, mære metodes leoht, myrgþ and tohiht eadgum and earmum, eallum brice.	Day, the glorious light of the Creator, is sent by the Lord; it is beloved of men, a source of hope and happiness to rich and poor, and of service to all.	Dawn, New Beginning, Future, Day, Dawn, Happiness, Success

The Anglo-Saxon Fuþorc and the Anglo-Saxon Rune Poem

No.	Rune	Name	Sound	Rune Poem	Translation	Divination Meanings
1	ᚠ	Feoh	/F/, [V]	Feoh byþ frofur fira gehwylcum; sceal ðeah manna gehwylc miclun hyt dælan gif he wile for drihtne domes hleotan.	Wealth is a comfort to all men; yet must every man bestow it freely, if he wish to gain honour in the sight of the Lord.	Profit, Prosperity, Money, Power, Wealth, Luck, Success, Happiness
2	ᚢ	Ūr	/U/, /U:/	Ur byþ anmod ond oferhyrned, felafrecne deor, feohteþ mid hornum mære morstapa; þæt is modig wuht.	The aurochs is proud and has great horns; it is a very savage beast and fights with its horns; a great ranger of the moors, it is a creature of mettle.	Strength, Energy, Stamina, Will, Strength, Speed, Desire, Gateway
3	ᚦ	Þorn	/Θ/, [Ð]	Ðorn byþ ðearle scearp; ðegna gehwylcum anfeng ys yfyl, ungemetum repe manna gehwelcum, ðe him mid resteð.	The thorn is exceedingly sharp, an evil thing for any knight to touch, uncommonly severe on all who sit among them.	Pain, Hindrance, Difficulties, Discipline, Meditation, Study
4	ᚩ	Ōs	/O/, /O:/	Os byþ ordfruma ælere spræce, wisdomes wraþu ond witena frofur and eorla gehwam eadnys ond tohiht.	The mouth is the source of all language, a pillar of wisdom and a comfort to wise men, a blessing and a joy to every knight.	Speech, Wisdom, Source, Connection, Communication, Mouth

No.	Rune	Name	Sound	Rune Poem	Translation	Divination Meanings
5	ᚱ	Rād	/R/	Rad byþ on recyde rinca gehwylcum sefte ond swiþhwæt, ðamðe sitteþ on ufan meare mægenheardum ofer milpaþas.	Riding seems easy to every warrior while he is indoors and very courageous to him who traverses the high-roads on the back of a stout horse.	Journey, Movement, Change, Orientation, Travel, Relocation, Dance of Life
6	ᚳ	Cēn	/K/, /Ki/, /TΣ/	Cen byþ cwicera gehwam, cuþ on fyre blac ond beorhtlic, byrneþ oftust ðær hi æþelingas inne restaþ.	The torch is known to every living man by its pale, bright flame; it always burns where princes sit within.	Fire, Wisdom, Enlightenment, Pain, Torch, Wisdom, Creativity
7	ᚷ	Gyfu	/g/, [Ɣ], /g/), /J/, /X/?, /Gi/	Gyfu gumena byþ gleng and herenys, wraþu and wyrþscype and wræcna gehwam ar and ætwist, ðe byþ oþra leas.	Generosity brings credit and honour, which support one's dignity; it furnishes help and subsistence to all broken men who are devoid of aught else.	Generosity, Friendship, Hospitality, Honour, Gifts, Relationship
8	ᚹ	Ƿynn	/W/	Wenne bruceþ, ðe can weana lyt sares and sorge and him sylfa hæfþ blæd and blysse and eac byrga geniht.	Bliss he enjoys who knows not suffering, sorrow nor anxiety, and has prosperity and happiness and a good enough house.	Happiness, Bliss, Love, Hope, Joy, Pleasure, Fellowship, Glory
9	ᚻ	Hægl	/H/, /X/, [Ç]	Hægl byþ hwitust corna; hwyrft hit of heofones lyfte, wealcaþ hit windes scura; weorþeþ hit to wætere syððan.	Hail is the whitest of grain; it is whirled from the vault of heaven and is tossed about by gusts of wind and then it melts into water.	Sudden Difficulties, Pain, Fortification, Hail, Drastic Change, Life Lessons

No.	Rune	Name	Sound	Rune Poem	Translation	Divination Meanings
10	ᚾ	Nyd	/N/	Nyd byþ nearu on breostan; weorþeþ hi þeah oft niþa bearnum to helpe and to hæle gehwæþre, gif hi his hlystaþ æror.	Trouble is oppressive to the heart; yet often it proves a source of help and salvation to the children of men, to everyone who heeds it betimes.	Trouble, Duress, Constraints, Necessity, Endurance, Survival, Determination, Patience
11	ᛁ	Īs	/I/, /I:/	Is byþ ofereald, ungemetum slidor, glisnaþ glæshluttur gimmum gelicust, flor forste geworuht, fæger ansyne.	Ice is very cold and immeasurably slippery; it glistens as clear as glass and most like to gems; it is a floor wrought by the frost, fair to look upon.	Cold, Hindrance, Immobility, Bridge, Challenge, reinforcement, Standoff
12	ᛄ	Gēr	/J/	Ger byÞ gumena hiht, ðonne God læteþ, halig heofones cyning, hrusan syllan beorhte bleda beornum ond ðearfum.	Summer is a joy to men, when God, the holy King of Heaven, suffers the earth to bring forth shining fruits for rich and poor alike.	Year, Earth, Harvest, Livelihood, Year, Change, Cycle, Reward
13	ᛇ	Ēoh	/I:/? /X/, [Ç]	Eoh byþ utan unsmeþe treow, heard hrusan fæst, hyrde fyres, wyrtrumun underwreþyd, wyn on eþle.	The yew is a tree with rough bark, hard and fast in the earth, supported by its roots, a guardian of flame and a joy upon an estate.	Endurance, Strength, Death, Creation, Transformation, Turning Point, Yew
14	ᛈ	Peorð	/P/	Peorð byþ symble plega and hlehter wlancum [on middum], ðar wigan sittaþ on beorsele bliþe ætsomne.	Peorth is a source of recreation and amusement to the great, where warriors sit blithely together in the banqueting-hall.	Joy, Feasting, Drinking Parties, Celebration, Mysteries, Secrets, Occult Abilities

No.	Rune	Name	Sound	Rune Poem	Translation	Divination Meanings
15	ᛉ	Eolhx	/KS/	Eolh-secg eard hæfþ oftust on fenne wexeð on wature, wundaþ grimme, blode breneð beorna gehwylcne ðe him ænigne onfeng gedeþ.	The Eolh-sedge is mostly to be found in a marsh; it grows in the water and makes a ghastly wound, covering with blood every warrior who touches it.	Death, Life, Protection, Protection, Support, Sanctuary
16	ᛋ	Sigel	/S/, [Z]	Sigel semannum symble biþ on hihte, ðonne hi hine feriaþ ofer fisces beþ, oþ hi brimhengest bringeþ to lande.	The sun is ever a joy in the hopes of seafarers when they journey away over the fishes' bath, until the courser of the deep bears them to land.	Guiding Light, Anchor, Life, Clockwork, Sun, Health, Energy, Power
17	ᛏ	Tī, tīr	/T/	Tir biþ tacna sum, healdeð trywa wel wiþ æþelingas; a biþ on færylde ofer nihta genipu, næfre swiceþ.	Tiw is a guiding star; well does it keep faith with princes; it is ever on its course over the mists of night and never fails.	Victory, Battle, Omen, Guide, Justice, Authority, Analysis, Rationality
18	ᛒ	Beorc	/B/	Beorc byþ bleda leas, bereþ efne swa ðeah tanas butan tudder, biþ on telgum wlitig, heah on helme hrysted fægere, geloden leafum, lyfte getenge.	The poplar bears no fruit; yet without seed it brings forth suckers, for it is generated from its leaves. Splendid are its branches and gloriously adorned its lofty crown which reaches to the skies.	Light, Renewal, Femininity, Fertilisation, Birth, Fertility, Growth, Liberation, Love Affair

No.	Rune	Name	Sound	Rune Poem	Translation	Divination Meanings
19	ᛖ	Eh	/E/, /E:/	Eh byþ for eorlum æþelinga wyn, hors hofum wlanc, ðær him hæleþ ymb[e] welege on wicgum wrixlaþ spræce and biþ unstyllum æfre frofur.	The horse is a joy to princes in the presence of warriors. A steed in the pride of its hoofs, when rich men on horseback bandy words about it; and it is ever a source of comfort to the restless.	Motion, Reliability, Connection, Destiny, Movement, Change, Harmony, Teamwork
20	ᛗ	Mann	/M/	Man byþ on myrgþe his magan leof: sceal þeah anra gehwylc oðrum swican, forðum drihten wyle dome sine þæt earme flæsc eorþan betæcan.	The joyous man is dear to his kinsmen; yet every man is doomed to fail his fellow, since the Lord by his decree will commit the vile carrion to the earth.	Mankind, Faithfulness, Companionship, Friendship, Self, Human Race, Social Order, Awareness
21	ᛚ	Lagu	/L/	Lagu byþ leodum langsum geþuht, gif hi sculun neþan on nacan tealtum and hi sæyþa swyþe bregaþ and se brimhengest bridles ne gym[eð].	The ocean seems interminable to men, if they venture on the rolling bark and the waves of the sea terrify them and the courser of the deep heed not its bridle.	Mutability, Flow, Mystery, Water, Life Energy, Imagination, Dreams
22	ᛜ/ᛝ	Ing	/NG/, /N/	Ing wæs ærest mid East-Denum gesewen secgun, oþ he siððan est ofer wæg gewat; wæn æfter ran; ðus Heardingas ðone hæle nemdun.	Ing was first seen by men among the East-Danes, till, followed by his chariot, he departed eastwards over the waves. So the Heardingas named the hero.	Forefather, Manhood, Seed, Consecration, Fertility, New Life, Completion

No.	Rune	Name	Sound	Rune Poem	Translation	Divination Meanings
23		Ēðel	/Ø/, /Ø:/	Eþel byþ oferleof æghwylcum men, gif he mot ðær rihtes and gerysena on brucan on bolde bleadum oftast.	An estate is very dear to every man, if he can enjoy there in his house whatever is right and proper in constant prosperity.	Family, Offspring, Home, Shelter, Heritage, Heirlooms, Land of Birth
24		Dæg	/D/	Dæg byþ drihtnes sond, deore mannum, mære metodes leoht, myrgþ and tohiht eadgum and earmum, eallum brice.	Day, the glorious light of the Creator, is sent by the Lord; it is beloved of men, a source of hope and happiness to rich and poor, and of service to all.	Dawn, New Beginning, Future, Day, Dawn, Happiness, Success
25		Āc	/ɑ/, /ɑ:/	Ac byþ on eorþan elda bearnum flæsces fodor, fereþ gelome ofer ganotes bæþ; garsecg fandaþ hwæþer ac hæbbe æþele treowe.	The oak fattens the flesh of pigs for the children of men. Often it traverses the gannet's bath, and the ocean proves whether the oak keeps faith in honourable fashion.	Order, Gods, Oak
26		Æsc	/Æ/, /Æ:/	Æsc biþ oferheah, eldum dyre stiþ on staþule, stede rihte hylt, ðeah him feohtan on firas monige.	The ash is exceedingly high and precious to men. With its sturdy trunk it offers a stubborn resistance, though attacked by many a man.	Order, Gods, Ash Tree

No.	Rune	Name	Sound	Rune Poem	Translation	Divination Meanings
27		Yr	/Y/, /Y:/	Yr byþ æþelinga and eorla gehwæs wyn and wyrþmynd, byþ on wicge fæger, fæstlic on færelde, fyrdgeatewa sum.	Yr is a source of joy and honour to every prince and knight; it looks well on a horse and is a reliable equipment for a journey.	Mastery, Skill, Knowledge, Yew Bow
28		Īor	/IO/?, /I:O:/?	Iar byþ eafix and ðeah a bruceþ fodres on foldan, hafaþ fægerne eard wætre beworpen, ðær he wynnum leofaþ.	Iar is a river fish and yet it always feeds on land; it has a fair abode encompassed by water, where it lives in happiness.	Serpent, Dual Nature, Hardships
29		Ēar	/Æɑ/, /Æ:ɑ/	Ear byþ egle eorla gehwylcun, ðonn[e] fæstlice flæsc onginneþ, hraw colian, hrusan ceosan blac to gebeddan; bleda gedreosaþ, wynna gewitaþ, wera geswicaþ.	The grave is horrible to every knight, when the corpse quickly begins to cool and is laid in the bosom of the dark earth. Prosperity declines, happiness passes away and covenants are broken.	Earth, Endings, Life and Death
30		Calc	/K/			Chalice, Endings
31		Gar, Gungnir	/K/G/, [Ɣ]			Gungnir, Spear of Odin
32		Cweorð	/K/KW			Fire, Flame, Transformation
33		Stan	/ST/			Stone, Obstructions

The Younger Fuþark and the Icelandic Rune Poem

No.	Rune	Name	Sound	Rune Poem	Translation	Divination Meanings

1	ᚠ	Fé	F/V	Fé er frænda róg
				  ok flæðar viti
				  ok grafseiðs gata
					Wealth = source of discord among kinsmen
					  and fire of the sea
					  and path of the serpent.
						Profit, Prosperity, Money, Power

2	ᚢ	Úr	U/W, Y, O, Ø	Úr er skýja grátr
				  ok skára þverrir
				  ok hirðis hatr.
					Shower = lamentation of the clouds
					  and ruin of the hay-harvest
					  and abomination of the shepherd.
						Shapelessness, Power, Chaos, Will

3	ᚦ	Þurs	Þ, Ð	Þurs er kvenna kvöl
				  ok kletta búi
				  ok varðrúnar verr.
					Giant = torture of women
					  and cliff-dweller
					  and husband of a giantess.
						Duress, Pain, Suffering, Protection

4	ᚬ	Óss	A, O, Æ	Óss er algingautr
				  ok ásgarðs jöfurr,
				  ok valhallar vísi.
					God = aged Gautr and prince of Ásgarðr
					  and lord of Vallhalla.
						Connection, Union, Wisdom, Wellspring

5	ᚱ	Reið	R	Reið er sitjandi sæla
				  ok snúðig ferð
				  ok jórs erfiði.
					Riding = joy of the horsemen
					  and speedy journey
					  and toil of the steed.
						Journey, Movement, Change, Orientation

6	ᚴ	Kaun	K, G	Kaun er barna böl
				  ok bardaga [för]
				  ok holdfúa hús.
					Ulcer = disease fatal to children
					  and painful spot
					  and abode of mortification.
						Pain, Misfortune, Learning, Sacrifice

7	ᚼ	Hagall	H	Hagall er kaldakorn
				  ok krapadrífa
				  ok snáka sótt.
					Hail = cold grain
					  and shower of sleet
					  and sickness of serpents.
						Sudden Difficulties, Pain, Cold, Fortification

8	ᚾ	Nauð	N	Nauð er Þýjar þrá
				  ok þungr kostr
				  ok vássamlig verk.
					Constraint = grief of the bond-maid
					  and state of oppression
					  and toilsome work.
						Dilemma, Duress, Restriction, Necessity

Runes
3. Meanings

No.	Rune	Name	Sound	Rune Poem	Translation	Divination Meanings
9	ᛁ	Íss	I, E	Íss er árbörkr ok unnar þak ok feigra manna fár.	Ice = bark of rivers and roof of the wave and destruction of the doomed.	Cold, Hindrance, Immobility, Bridge
10	ᛏ	Ár	A, Æ, E	Ár er gumna góði ok gott sumar algróinn akr.	Plenty = boon to men and good summer and thriving crops.	Year, Earth, Harvest, Prosperity
11	ᛋ	Sól	S	Sól er skýja skjöldr ok skínandi röðull ok ísa aldrtregi.	Sun = shield of the clouds and shining ray and destroyer of ice.	Beacon, Anchor, Life, Clockwork
12	ᛏ	Týr	T, D	Týr er einhendr áss ok ulfs leifar ok hofa hilmir.	Týr = god with one hand and leavings of the wolf and prince of temples.	Victory, Battle, Upkeep, Guide
13	ᛒ	Bjarkan	B, P	Bjarkan er laufgat lim ok lítit tré ok ungsamligr viðr.	Birch = leafy twig and little tree and fresh young shrub.	Light, Renewal, Femininity, Fertilisation
14	ᛘ	Maðr	M	Maðr er manns gaman ok moldar auki ok skipa skreytir.	Man = delight of man and augmentation of the earth and adorner of ships.	Mankind, Loyalty, Company, Friendship
15	ᛚ	Lögr	L	Lögr er vellanda vatn ok viðr ketill ok glömmungr grund.	Water = eddying stream and broad geysir and land of the fish.	Mutability, Flow, Life, Mystery
16	ᛦ	Ýr	R	Ýr er bendr bogi ok brotgjarnt járn ok fífu fárbauti.	Yew = bent bow and brittle iron and giant of the arrow.	Endurance, Strength, Death, Creation

The Icelandic Fuþark and the Late Icelandic Rune Poem

No.	Rune	Name	Sound	Rune Poem	Translation	Divination Meanings

1	ᚠ	Fé	F	Fé er frænda róg
				  ok flæðar viti
				  ok grafseiðs gata
					Wealth is a source of discord among kinsmen
					  and fire of the sea
					  and path of the serpent.
						Profit, Prosperity, Money, Power

2	ᚢ	Úr	U, Ú, V	Úr er skýja grátr
				  ok skára þverrir
				  ok hirðis hatr.
					Shower is the lamentation of the clouds
					  and ruin of the hay-harvest
					  and abomination of the shepherd.
						Rain, Fog, Shapelessness, Power

3	þ	Þurs	Þ, Ð, D	Þurs er kvenna kvöl
				  ok kletta búi
				  ok varðrúnar verr.
					Giant is a torture of women
					  and cliff-dweller
					  and husband of a giantess.
						Duress, Pain, Suffering, Protection

4	ᚫ	Óss	O, Ó	Óss er algingautr
				  ok ásgarðs jöfurr,
				  ok valhallar vísi.
					God is aged Gautr and prince of Ásgarðr
					  and lord of Vallhalla.
						Connection, Synthesis, Wisdom, Source

5	ᚱ	Reið	R	Reið er sitjandi sæla
				  ok snúðig ferð
				  ok jórs erfiði.
					Riding is the joy of the horsemen
					  and speedy journey
					  and toil of the steed.
						Journey, Movement, Change, Orientation

6	ᚴ	Kaun	K	Kaun er barna böl
				  ok bardaga [för]
				  ok holdfúa hús.
					Ulcer is a disease fatal to children
					  and painful spot
					  and abode of mortification.
						Pain, Wound, Misfortune, Learning

7	ᚴ̇	Stunginn Kaun	G	Stunginn kaun stofnar mæði stór sár trú ég blæði	Stunginn Kaun causes exhaustion great wounds, I believe, will bleed.	Wound, Betrayal, Exhaustion, Death

8	ᚼ	Hagall	H	Hagall er kaldakorn
				  ok krapadrífa
				  ok snáka sótt.
					Hail is cold grain and shower of sleet
					  and sickness of serpents.
						Sudden difficulties, Pain, Cold, Fortification

No.	Rune	Name	Sound	Rune Poem	Translation	Divination Meanings
9	ᚼ	Nauð	N	Nauð er Þýjar þrá ok þungr kostr ok vássamlig verk.	Constraint is the grief of the bond-maid and state of oppression and toilsome work.	Longing, Problem, Duress, Necessity
10	ᛁ	Íss	I, Í, Y, Ý	Íss er árbörkr ok unnar þak ok feigra manna fár.	Ice is the bark of rivers and roof of the wave and destruction of the doomed.	Cold, Hindrance, Immobility, Bridge
11	┼	Stunginn Ís	E, É	Stunginn ís stendur reyndur stuldur oft er leyndur	Stunginn Ís stands tested, Theft is often hidden.	Hole in Ice, Provisions, Thaw, Hidden Danger
12	ᛅ	Ár	A, Á	Ár er gumna góði ok gott sumar algróinn akr.	Ár is boon to men and good summer and thriving crops.	Year, Earth, Crops, Livelihood
13	ᛋ	Sól	S	Sól er skýja skjöldr ok skínandi röðull ok ísa aldrtregi.	Sun is the shield of the clouds and shining ray and destroyer of ice.	Guiding Light, Anchor, Life, Clockwork
14	ᛌ	Knésól	Z, X, C	Knésól kallar reina kemur í stríði skeina	Knésól calls horses Harm comes in battle	Sunset, Grief, Wolf, New Beginning
15	ᛏ	Týr	T	Týr er einhendr áss ok ulfs leifar ok hofa hilmir.	Týr is the god with one hand and leavings of the wolf and prince of temples.	Victory, Sacrifice, Courage, Strength
16	ᛐ	Stunginn Týr	Ð, D	Stunginn Tyr særður ásinn djarfi sá var í víga starfi	Pierced Tyr, bold injured god He was in the midst of battle.	Death, Grief, Misfortune, Destiny
17	ᛐ	Dís	Ð, D	Dís er ein af nornunum, Notandi fornaldar	Dís is one of norns, User of ancient sorcery	Destiny, Sorcery, Old Age, Lifetime

No.	Rune	Name	Sound	Rune Poem	Translation	Divination Meanings
18	ᛒ	Bjarkan	B	Bjarkan er laufgat lim ok lítit tré ok ungsamligr viðr.	Birch is a leafy twig and little tree and fresh young shrub.	Light, Renewal, Femininity, Fertilisation
19	ᛔ	Plástur	P	Plástur er meina mýkt manna græðing og benja bót	A bandage is pain's dulling, Man's healing, And injuries remedied.	Light, Renewal, Femininity, Fertilisation
20	ᛘ	Maðr	M	Maðr er manns gaman ok moldar auki ok skipa skreytir.	Man is a delight of man, and augmentation of the earth, and adorner of ships.	Mankind, Loyalty, Friendship, Advancement
21	ᛚ	Lögr	L	Lögr er vellanda vatn ok viðr ketill ok glömmungr grund.	Water is an eddying stream, and broad geysir, and land of the fish.	Flow, Difficult Roads, Life, Mystery
22	ᛦ	Ýr	Y, Ý, Ö	Ýr er bendr bogi ok brotgjarnt járn ok fífu fárbauti.	Yew is a bent bow, and brittle iron, and giant of the arrow.	Endurance, Strength, Toil, Death
23	ᛇ	Æsa	Æ	Heift er öllum óhrein, Barn öskrar, dæmir pyndingar.	Fury is unclean to all, A child screams, doom tortures.	Destiny, Mother, Gift, Death
24	ᛯ	Elli	Z	Elli hvíld erfiði og elli ei vill vera á felli	Old age, rest, toil and age, no want to be on a mountain.	Old Age, Difficulties, End of Life, Care

4. Divination

Divination is an attempt to gain insight into the will and intentions of the divine and the many forces operating around us that influence and shape our lives.

The person who wishes to have their query answered is called the 'Querent'.

The method of selecting or casting the runes is decided upon by the 'reader', who could also be the Querent asking for themselves.

There is some difference of opinion on whether or not to take account of the rotational position of the rune when drawn. Some say that there is a different meaning when the rune is upside down or 'reversed'. However, when some runes are reversed they read the same.

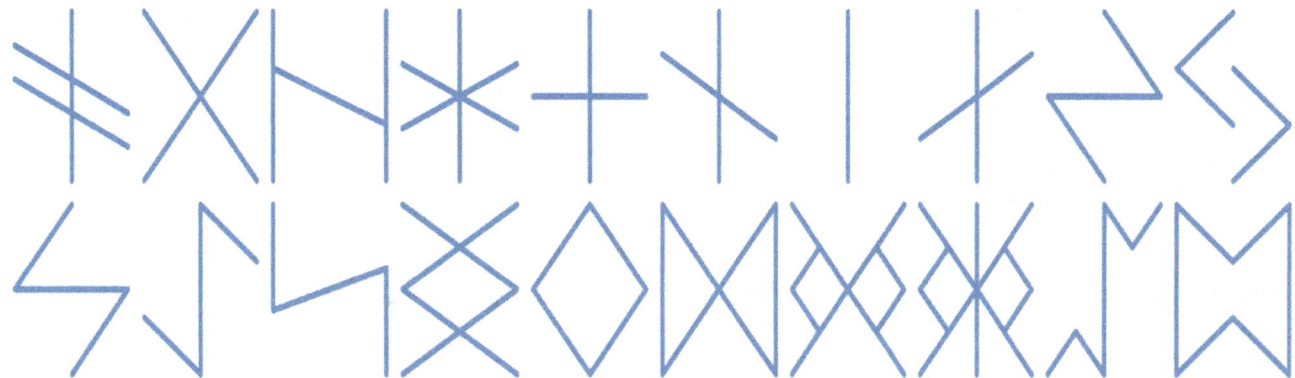

If however the reader does decide to take into account the rotational position of the rune, then there follows the issue of at what point we consider a rune to be reversed.

If the rune in question is rotated more than 90 degrees in either direction away from its perfect vertical position, it can be said to be reversed.

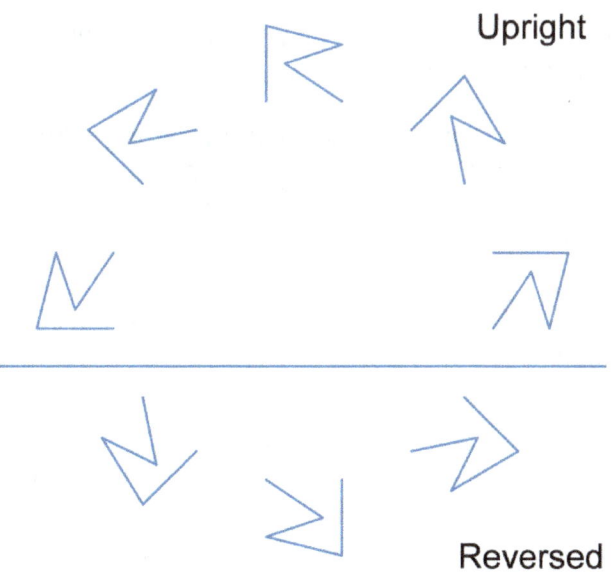

For interpretation of the runes in the context of their spread or casting, it is worth remembering that the Fuþark is commonly arranged into three rows called Ætt (singular) or Ættir (plural), from the Old Norse '*Átt*' or '*Ætt*' meaning 'dynasty', 'lineage', 'generation', 'family', or 'language'.

Ætt 1 - Freyja's Ætt

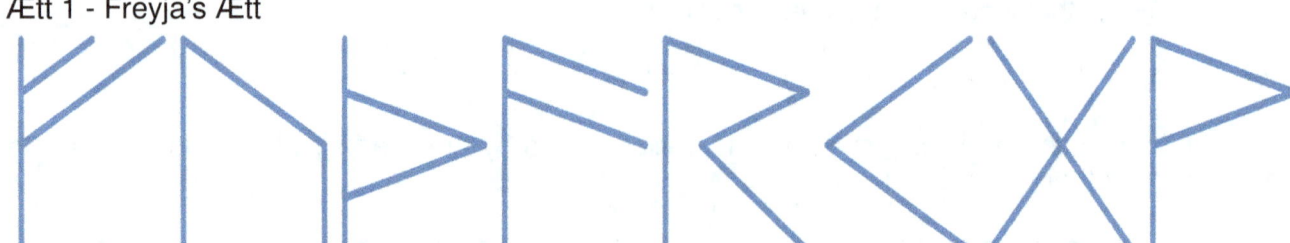

The forces of creation, earth, the emergence of order from chaos, nurturing, positive.
Meaning / answer: positive, yes, simple, maybe, clear, possibility, beginning

Ætt 2 - Hagal / Heimdall's Ætt

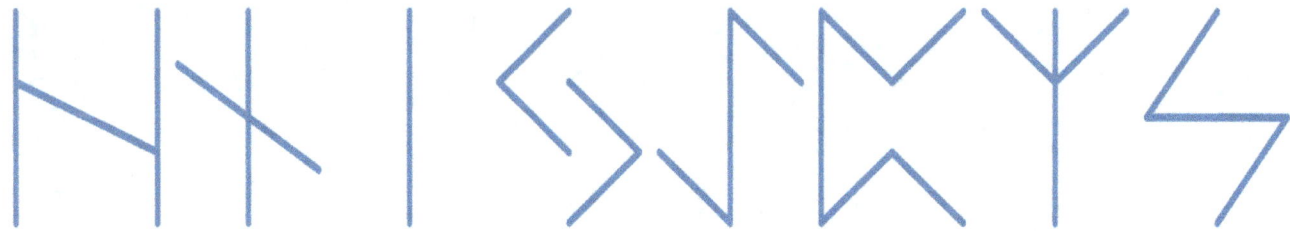

The forces of disruption, trial, chaos and change, dynamic powers of transformation.
Meaning / answer: negative, no, mixed, maybe not, unclear, disruption, conflict

Ætt 3 - Tyr's Ætt

Divine forces, the function of fate, divine intervention, atonement, spiritual transformation.
Meaning / answer: negative, no, mixed, maybe not, unclear, sacrifice, conclusion

So it is possible to take note of which of the Ættir each rune comes from in each 'spread' or 'casting', then interpreting those as beginnings, conflicts or trials, and endings or conclusions regardless of where they appear.

The One Rune Reading

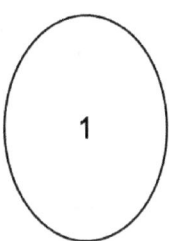

Ask a closed or 'Yes' or 'No' question.
Note the Ætt that the rune is from for an answer.

or

Ask an open or general question.
Look to the meaning of the individual rune.

The Three Rune Spread

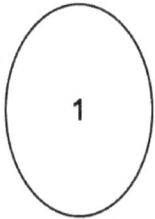 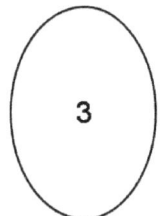

| Past (Urðr) | Present (Verðandi) | Future (Skuld) |

Cause — Effect — Solution

Action — Challenge — Overview

The Hidden Truth Spread

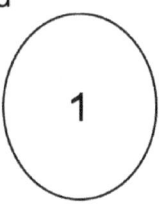 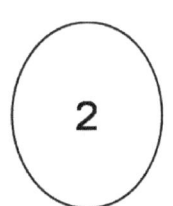

What is the truth behind this situation? — How does this affect me?

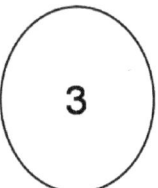 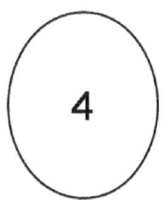

Why has this been hidden from me? — How do I deal with this new information?

The Five Rune Spread

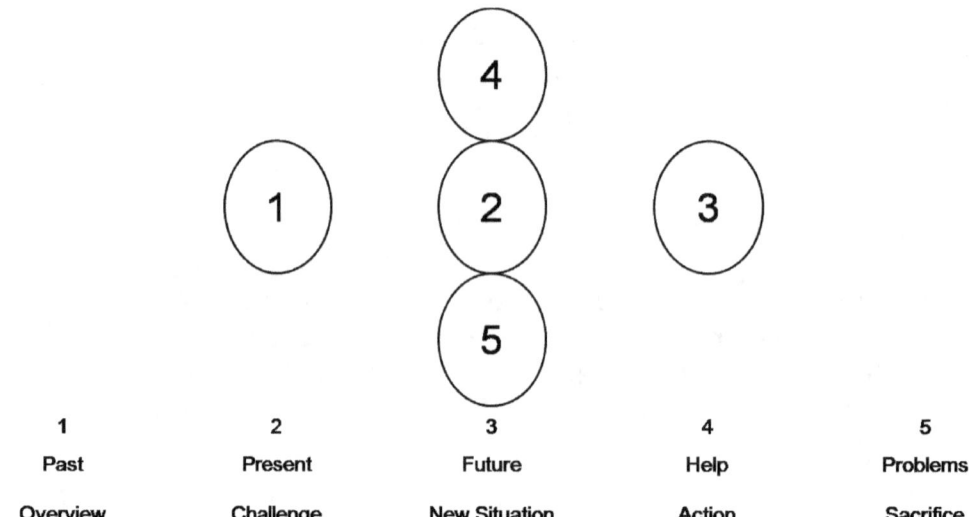

1	2	3	4	5
Past	Present	Future	Help	Problems
Overview	Challenge	New Situation	Action	Sacrifice

The Runic V

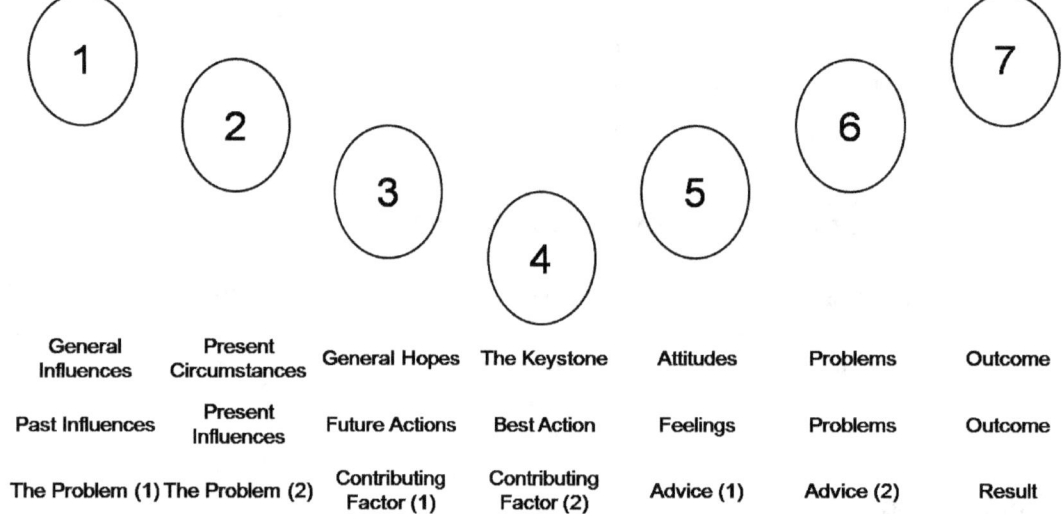

General Influences	Present Circumstances	General Hopes	The Keystone	Attitudes	Problems	Outcome
Past Influences	Present Influences	Future Actions	Best Action	Feelings	Problems	Outcome
The Problem (1)	The Problem (2)	Contributing Factor (1)	Contributing Factor (2)	Advice (1)	Advice (2)	Result

54

The Celtic Cross Spread

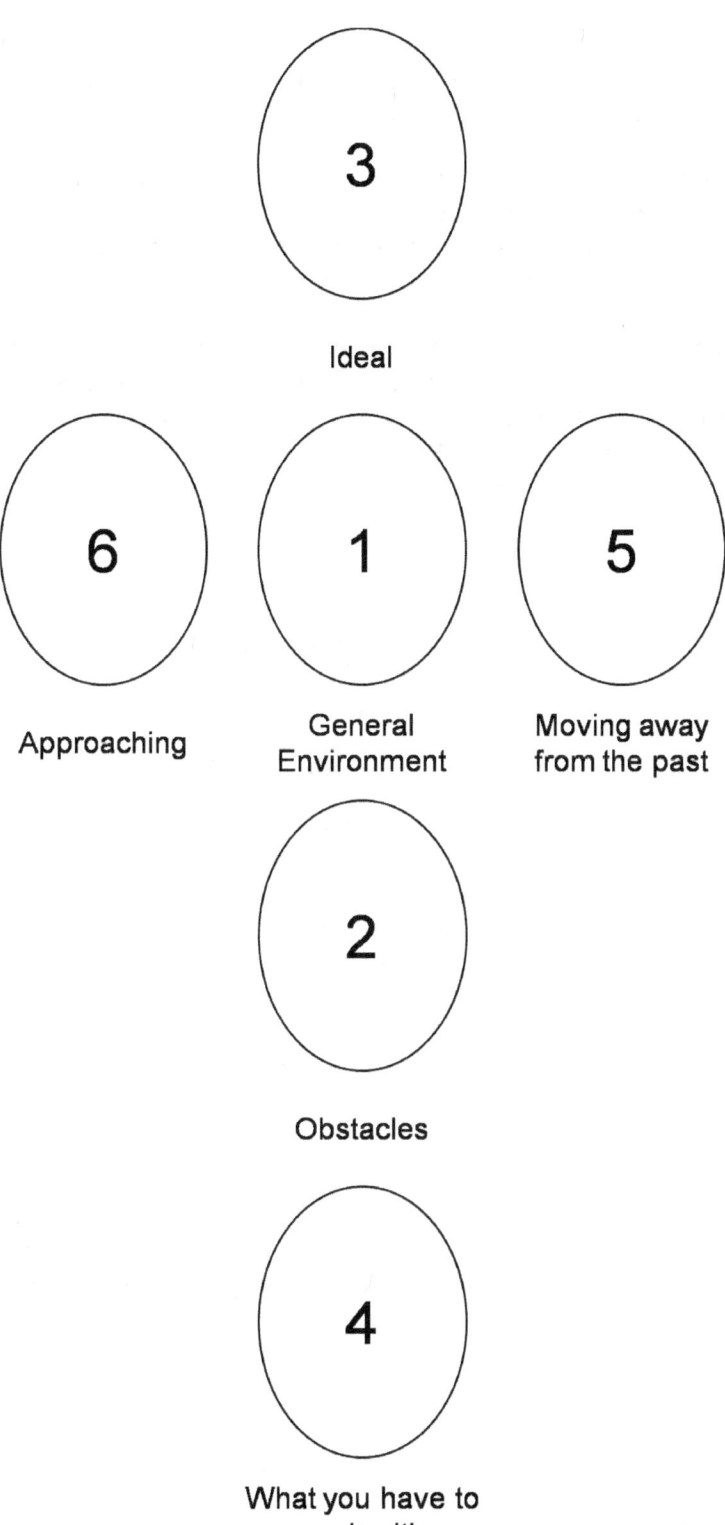
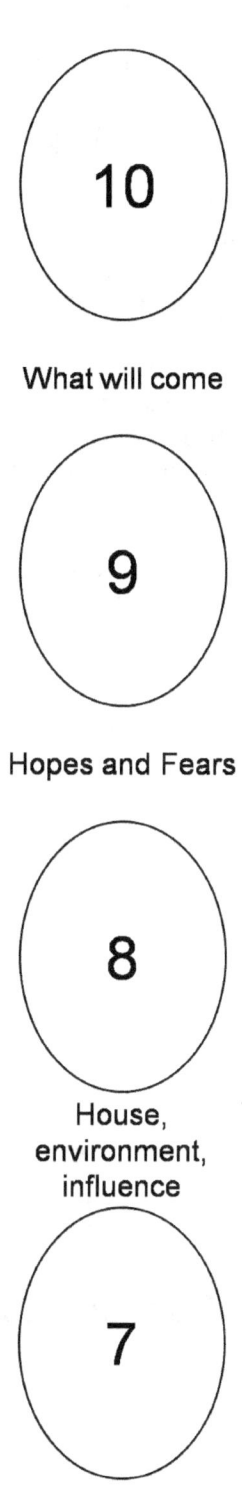

Rune Casting

The object of rune casting is to gather a small amount of runes at random from their rune pouch while meditating on the question or issue, and then casting the runes over the cloth letting them land where they may, and then interpreting the constellation of meaning that they create.

Once the runes have landed, any of the runes that are face down are turned the right way up. If you are taking note of the reversal of runes, take care when turning the rune the right way up, by turning it on its horizontal axis rather than its vertical one, or the rune and its meaning will be reversed. This works best if your runes are flat and regular in shape, otherwise this may not be possible.

A white cloth or material is preferable because it allows you to see the runes and the shape of how they have landed more clearly. The cloth can be marked with inner and outer circles representing the distant and close matters, with the centre of the circle representing now. Compass points as indicated below can provide a cross-section of issues from positive to negative, and past, present, and future.

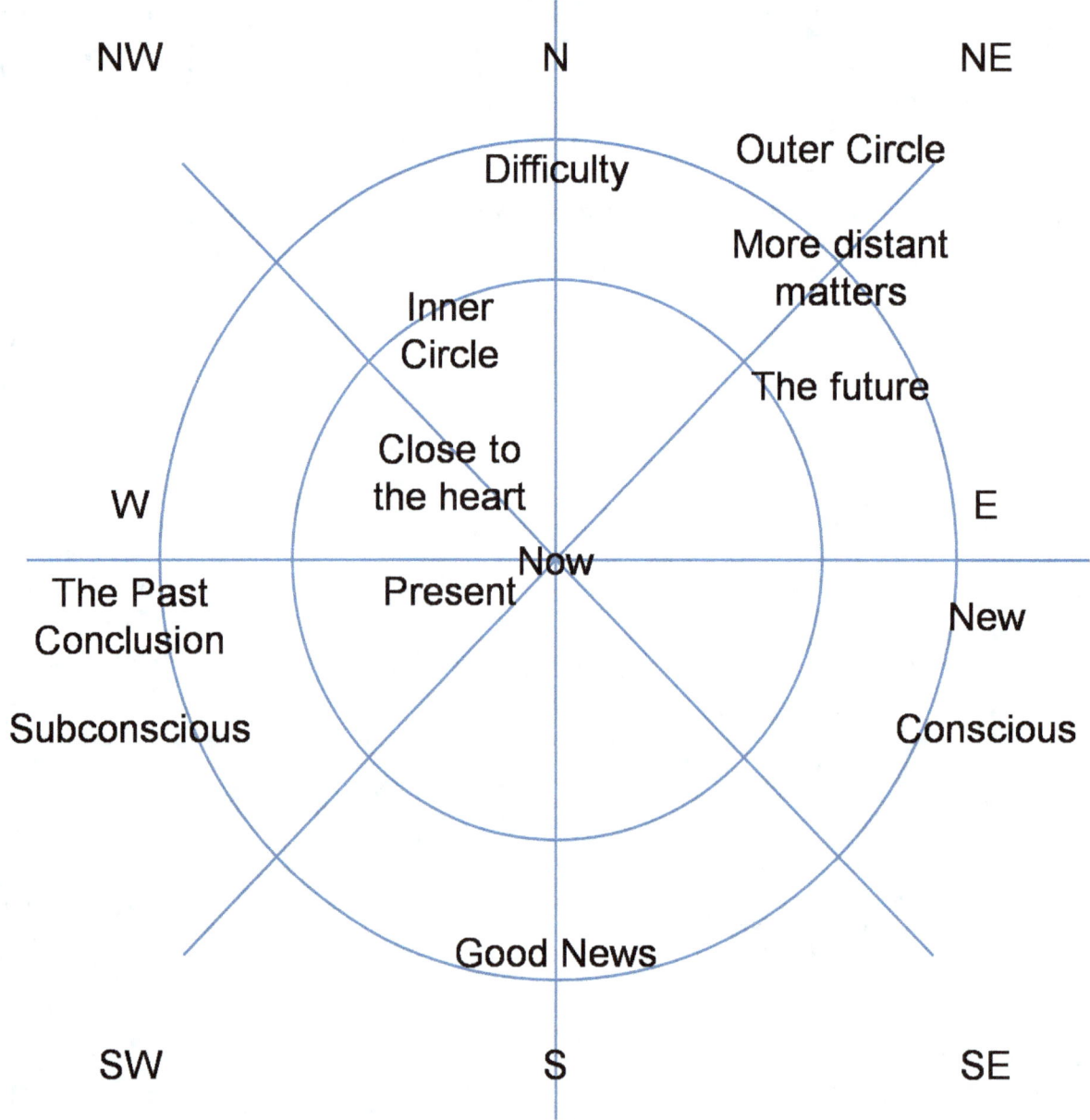

5. Magic

Magic works because we believe that it works. We believe in the process of signalling and communicating our intentions and desirable outcomes to the forces around us, releasing them into the universe, and having the confidence and belief to make it happen.

Whereas in divination we use the runes to ascertain the will and intention of forces around us, in rune magic we create our desired rune reading, and will it into being. We program the reading that we would wish to have.

Placing

You can place the rune or runes around your shrine or in an equally special space.
You can place runes where you would wish them to work, i.e. over a doorway for protection, etc.
You can wear runes as talismans or pendants or in your clothing or carry them with you.

Activating

You can use candles to light up the runes and to signal your desires and intentions.
You can use incense to help carry those intentions into the air.
You can use the power of the moon, a powerful symbolic embodiment of dreams and desires by placing your intentions on the night of a new moon, and then reviewing the outcome and success on the night of the following full moon.
You can whisper or chant the names of the runes you are using during meditation or ritual.

Maintaining

You can maintain your runes by:
- Placing them in water and leaving them over night.
- Placing them under the light of a full moon.
- Passing them one by one over incense smoke.
- Whispering or chanting the name of each rune.

The following tables describe the different ways in which runes can be used for magical purposes, including the Elder Fuþark, the Younger Fuþark, and the Icelandic Fuþark.

The Elder Fuþark

No.	Elder Rune	Elder Name	Magical Uses
1	ᚠ	Fehu	Energy projection and sending energy, drawing energy, increasing wealth, protecting valuables, increasing libido
2	ᚢ	Ūruz	Initiation, healing, shaping and forming of desire, will, knowledge of the self
3	ᚦ	Thurisaz	New beginnings, luck in circumstances beyond your control, guarding and protection, awakening the magical will
4	ᚨ	Ansuz	Magical incantation, convincing and magnetic speech, gaining wisdom, and divine communication, finding the truth in the matter, increasing magical energies
5	ᚱ	Raidō	Moral justice, rhythm and timing, ordered movement, travel
6	ᚲ	Kenaz / Kaunan	Protection from and healing of wounds, love, stability and passion in relationships, releases spirit into the realms of power, protection of valuables
7	ᚷ	Gebō	Love magic, endless exchange of energy and magical powers, mystical union, binding, a gift for a gift, karmic payback
8	ᚹ	Wunjō	Personal happiness and fulfilment, healing relationships, success in travel
9	ᚺ	Hagalaz	Completeness and bringing into being, warding, protection, luck, encouraging a positive result
10	ᚾ	Nauthiz / Naudiz	Overcoming fate and stress, developing magical will, sudden inspiration and inner might, achieving goals, to find a lover or to encourage a relationship
11	ᛁ	Isa / Īsaz	Strengthening concentration and will, maintaining something as it is, binding, holding on to something, halting movement
12	ᛃ	Jēra	Patience and natural harmony of magical will, spiritual understanding, creative planning, interactions with nature and natural time cycles, promoting healing
13	ᛇ	Īhwaz / Eihwaz	Initiation, wisdom from past lives, increasing power and store power, spirit communication, removal of obstacles
14	ᛈ	Perthro / Perth	Divination, perception of fate, to manifest magical intent, use when dealing with matters of speculation, finding lost things, good mental health

No.	Elder Rune	Elder Name	Magical Uses
15	ᛉ	Algiz	Protection from evil and enemies, strengthening luck and life force, communication and connection with guardian spirit, spiritual cleansing, strengthen magical power, travelling through other worlds, astral travel
16	ᛋ	Sōwilō	Strengthening magical spiritual will, guardianship and guidance, personal triumph, success, healing, increasing strength and self confidence
17	ᛏ	Tīwaz / Teiwaz	Victory and justice, strength in competition, defence magic, to strengthen with spiritual and moral force
18	ᛒ	Berkano / Berkanan	Fertility magic, protection, concealment and secrecy, family matters, to bring into being
19	ᛖ	Ehwaz	Bringing swift change, safe travel, shamanic totem animal, mystical wisdom, projecting and linking magical thoughts, cooperation
20	ᛗ	Mannaz	Strengthening all matters of the mind and psychic ability, balanced through meditation, increasing mental power and memory, to gain help from others
21	ᛚ	Laguz	Increasing and filling yourself with life-force and intuition, probing the subconscious and the unknown, physical and magical strength and vitality
22	ᛜ	Ingwaz	Storing, transferring or releasing magical power and energy, to keep a thing hidden, fertility, to bring a satisfactory conclusion
23	ᛟ	Ōthila / Ōthala	Strengthening the clan, family including spiritual ancestry, to gain past life wisdom, talents, to gain wealth and protect what you own, to protect the health of an elderly person
24	ᛞ	Dagaz	Becoming one with the universe through mystical inspiration, a change of attitude in yourself or someone else, synthesis of opposites into a single concept such as light and dark, financial increase

The Younger Fuþark

No.	Symbol	Name	Magical Uses
1	ᚠ	Fé	Energy projection and sending energy, drawing energy, increasing wealth, protecting valuables, increasing libido
2	ᚢ	Úr	Initiation, healing, shaping and forming of desire, will, knowledge of the self
3	ᚦ	Þurs	New beginnings, luck in circumstances beyond your control, guarding and protection, awakening the magical will
4	ᚬ	Óss	Magical incantation, convincing and magnetic speech, gaining wisdom, and divine communication, finding the truth in the matter, increasing magical energies
5	ᚱ	Reið	Moral justice, rhythm and timing, ordered movement, travel
6	ᚴ	Kaun	Protection from and healing of wounds, love, stability and passion in relationships, releases spirit into the realms of power, protection of valuables
7	ᚼ	Hagall	Completeness and bringing into being, warding, protection, luck, encouraging a positive result
8	ᚾ	Nauð	Overcoming fate and stress, developing magical will, sudden inspiration and inner might, achieving goals, to find a lover or to encourage a relationship
9	ᛁ	Íss	Strengthening concentration and will, maintaining something as it is, binding, holding on to something, halting movement
10	ᛅ	Ár	Patience and natural harmony of magical will, spiritual understanding, creative planning, interactions with nature and natural time cycles, promoting healing
11	ᛋ	Sól	Strengthening magical spiritual will, guardianship and guidance, personal triumph, success, healing, increasing strength and self confidence
12	ᛏ	Týr	Victory and justice, strength in competition, defence magic, to strengthen with spiritual and moral force
13	ᛒ	Bjarkan	Fertility magic, protection, concealment and secrecy, family matters, to bring into being
14	ᛘ	Maðr	Strengthening all matters of the mind and psychic ability, balanced through meditation, increasing mental power and memory, to gain help from others

No.	Symbol	Name	Magical Uses
15	ᛚ	Lögr	Increasing and filling yourself with life-force and intuition, probing the subconscious and the unknown, physical and magical strength and vitality
16	ᛦ	Ýr	Protection from evil and enemies, strengthening luck and life force, communication and connection with guardian spirit, spiritual cleansing, strengthen magical power, travelling through other worlds, astral travel

Runes   5. Magic

The Icelandic Fuþark

No.	Symbol	Name	Magical Uses
1	ᚠ	Fé	Energy projection and sending energy, drawing energy, increasing wealth, protecting valuables, increasing libido
2	ᚢ	Úr	Initiation, healing, shaping and forming of desire, will, knowledge of the self
3	ᚦ	Þurs	New beginnings, luck in circumstances beyond your control, guarding and protection, awakening the magical will
4	ᚬ	Óss	Magical incantation, convincing and magnetic speech, gaining wisdom, and divine communication, finding the truth in the matter, increasing magical energies
5	ᚱ	Reið	Moral justice, rhythm and timing, ordered movement, travel
6	ᚴ	Kaun	Protection from and healing of wounds, love, stability and passion in relationships, releases spirit into the realms of power, protection of valuables
7	ᚴ̇	Stunginn Kaun	Protection from and healing of wounds, love, stability and passion in relationships, releases spirit into the realms of power, protection of valuables
8	ᚼ	Hagall	Completeness and bringing into being, warding, protection, luck, encouraging a positive result
9	ᚾ	Nauð	Overcoming fate and stress, developing magical will, sudden inspiration and inner might, achieving goals, to find a lover or to encourage a relationship
10	ᛁ	Íss	Strengthening concentration and will, maintaining something as it is, binding, holding on to something, halting movement
11	ᛂ	Stunginn Ís	To thaw a freeze, to navigate difficult and bleak conditions
12	ᛅ	Ár	Patience and natural harmony of magical will, spiritual understanding, creative planning, interactions with nature and natural time cycles, promoting healing
13	ᛋ	Sól	Strengthening magical spiritual will, guardianship and guidance, personal triumph, success, healing, increasing strength and self confidence
14	ᛌ	Knésól	Survival, rebirth and re-creation

No.	Symbol	Name	Magical Uses
15	↑	Týr	Victory and justice, strength in competition, defence magic, to strengthen with spiritual and moral force
16		Stunginn Týr	Renewal, regeneration, re-initiation
17		Dís	Sorcery, Magic Arts
18	ᛒ	Bjarkan	Fertility magic, protection, concealment and secrecy, family matters, to bring into being
19		Plástur	Care, Relief, Remedy, Healing, Curing of Wounds, Amelioration of the Mind
20	ᛉ	Maðr	Comfort, Voice, Wordsmithery, Poetry
21	ᛚ	Lögr	Increasing and filling yourself with life-force and intuition, probing the subconscious and the unknown, physical and magical strength and vitality
22		Ýr	Death initiation, wisdom from past lives, increasing power and store power, spirit communication
23		Æsa	Nourishment, Longevity, Survival
24		Elli	Longevity, Sanctuary, Surviving Difficulty

6. Bindrunes

A bindrune is a combination of two or more runes into a single symbol, by varying degrees of overlapping and symmetrical configuration, to compound and amplify meaning and significance. It can be used to either exaggerate or obscure the meanings of the symbols used.

Example:

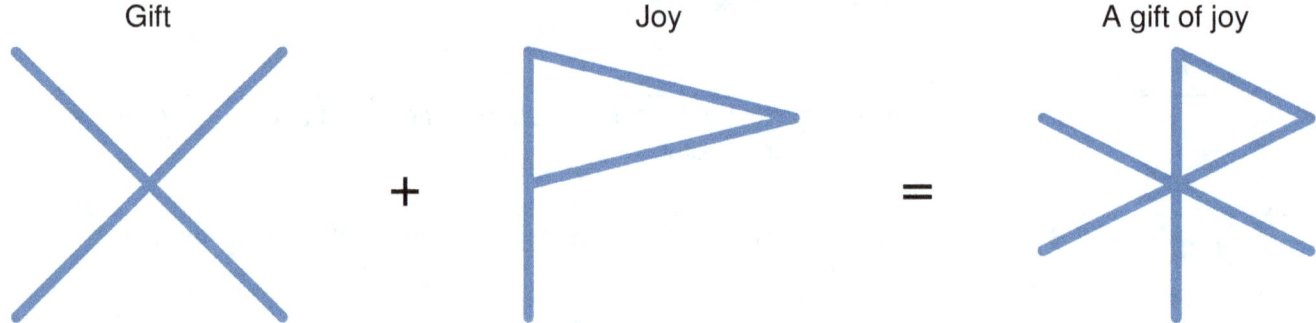

Make sure that while you are combining runes into bindrunes, there are no unintended runes that can also be inadvertently found that could undo or work against what the symbol represents.

Example:

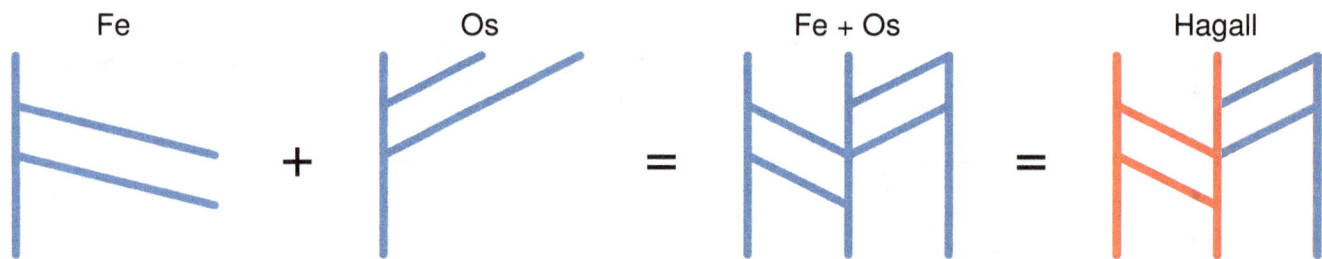

There is no limit to how many runes can be combined into a bindrune, or to the number of points of symmetry you can use, from a simple overlap of two runes, to large elaborate and intricate staves.

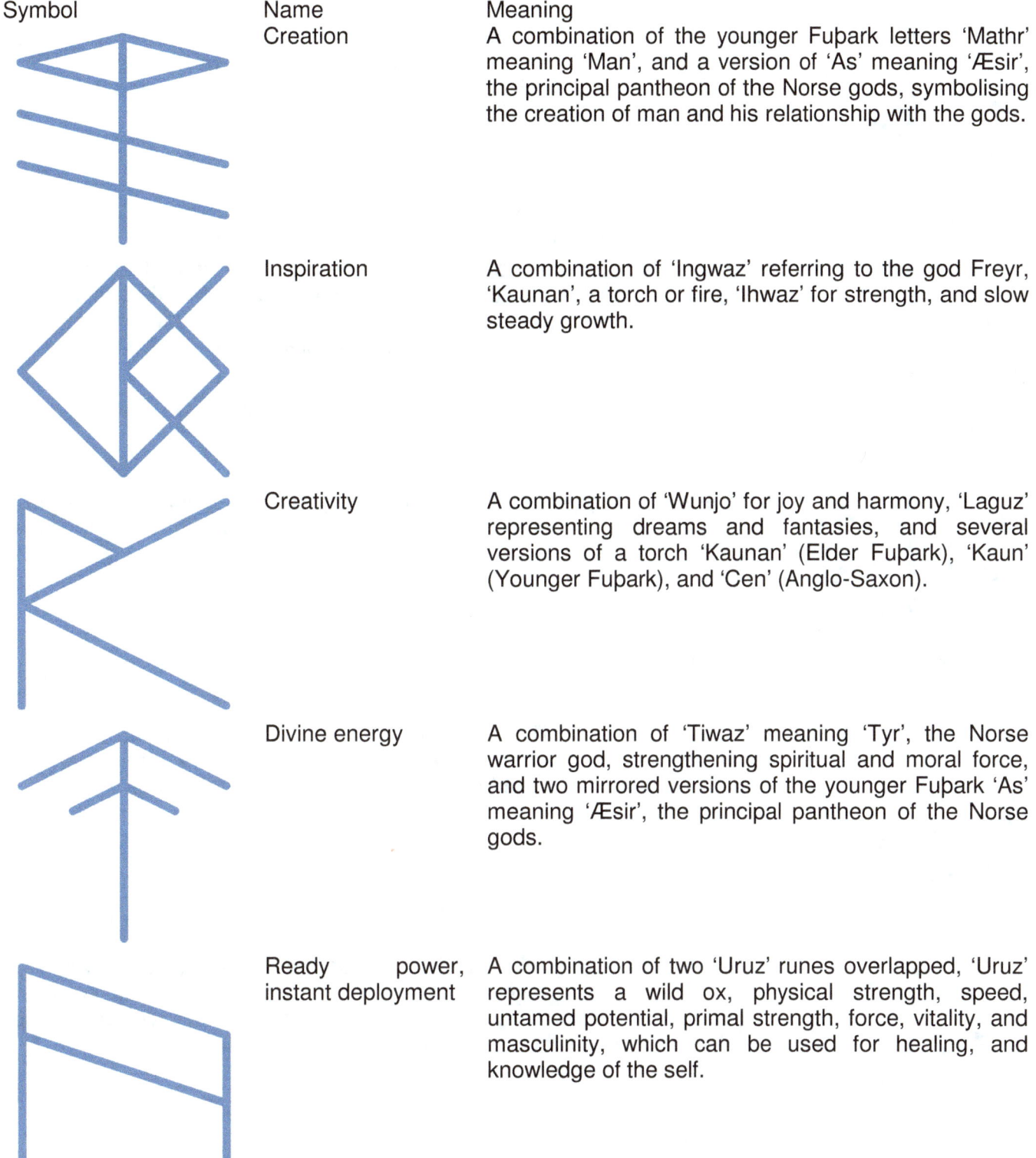

Symbol	Name	Meaning
	Creation	A combination of the younger Fuþark letters 'Mathr' meaning 'Man', and a version of 'As' meaning 'Æsir', the principal pantheon of the Norse gods, symbolising the creation of man and his relationship with the gods.
	Inspiration	A combination of 'Ingwaz' referring to the god Freyr, 'Kaunan', a torch or fire, 'Ihwaz' for strength, and slow steady growth.
	Creativity	A combination of 'Wunjo' for joy and harmony, 'Laguz' representing dreams and fantasies, and several versions of a torch 'Kaunan' (Elder Fuþark), 'Kaun' (Younger Fuþark), and 'Cen' (Anglo-Saxon).
	Divine energy	A combination of 'Tiwaz' meaning 'Tyr', the Norse warrior god, strengthening spiritual and moral force, and two mirrored versions of the younger Fuþark 'As' meaning 'Æsir', the principal pantheon of the Norse gods.
	Ready power, instant deployment	A combination of two 'Uruz' runes overlapped, 'Uruz' represents a wild ox, physical strength, speed, untamed potential, primal strength, force, vitality, and masculinity, which can be used for healing, and knowledge of the self.

Symbol	Name	Meaning
	Energy	A combination of the rune 'Raido', movement or movement of energy, and a version of the younger Fuþark 'As' meaning 'Æsir', the principal pantheon of the Norse gods.
	Fertility, taking root, beginning growth	A combination of 'Ihwaz', a tree and slow steady growth, 'Ehwaz', change and team work, and 'Dagaz', dawn, a breakthrough, awakening, embarking on an enterprise, and new beginnings.
	Growth and fertility	A combination of the younger Fuþark 'Yr', a yew tree or slow steady growth, and 'Bjarken', a birch tree, birth, fertility, growth, and bringing into being.
	Happy family and marriage	This is an overlapping of several 'Hagalaz' runes, which can be used for magical purposes for completeness, bringing into being, and warding or protection.
	Balanced joy	This is a double image of the 'Wunjo' rune, with one acting as the mirror of the other, meaning joy, comfort, pleasure, good fortune, delight, happiness, fellowship, and harmony.

Symbol	Name	Meaning
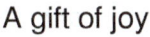	A gift of joy	This is a combination of the rune 'Gebo' meaning gift, and 'Wunjo' meaning joy (square version).
	A gift of joy	This is a combination of the rune 'Gebo' meaning gift, and 'Wunjo' meaning joy (hexagonal version).
	Lasting partnership	This is a combination of the rune 'Ingwaz', meaning internal growth, love, caring, and gentleness, and the rune 'Isaz' for binding together.
	Longevity and perseverance	This is a combination of the rune 'Dagaz', breakthrough or embarking on an enterprise, with the rune 'Isaz' for binding.
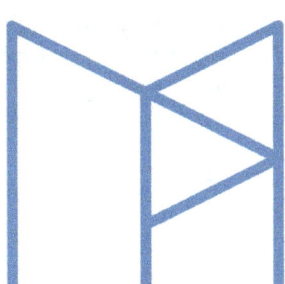	Enhancing athletic performance	This is a combination of the rune 'Ehwaz', physical movement, 'Uruz', physical strength, speed, untamed potential and vitality, and 'Sowilo', the sun, success, goals realised, honour, perfection, and health.

Symbol	Name	Meaning
	Good health	This is a combination of 'Laguz' meaning water and the power of renewal and healing, also increasing and filling yourself with a life force, and physical and magical strength, and 'Thurisaz' used for protection and warding.
	Grace and gracefulness	This is a combination of the rune 'Wunjo' meaning joy and harmony, and a version of the younger Fuþark 'As' meaning 'Æsir', the principal pantheon of the Norse gods.
	Health & healing	This is a combination of 'Laguz', water, the power of renewal, and healing, 'Berkano', renewal and rebirth, and 'Algiz' meaning a shield of protection.
	Health & healing	This is a combination of 'Kenaz', vital fire of life, 'Ihwaz', strength and reliability, and 'Sowilo', perfect health, all is well.
	Help giving up bad habits	This is a combination of 'Othala', where your heart lies, 'Kenaz', the vital fire of life and determination, and 'Jera', patience, natural harmony of magical will.

Symbol	Name	Meaning
	Medical healing	This is a combination of 'Berkano', renewal, nurturing, 'Algiz', strengthening protection, and 'Laguz', the power of renewal and healing.
	Personal good health	A combination of the rune 'Raido', movement or movement of energy, two 'Isaz' binding verticals, and a version of the younger Fuþark 'As' meaning 'Æsir', the principal pantheon of the Norse gods.
	Restoring balance	'Ansuz', divine communication, finding the truth, 'Algiz', communication and connection with a guardian spirit, spiritual cleansing, and 'Ehwaz', harmony, soul travel, a shamanic totem, and overcoming of obstacles.
	Vitality	This is a combination of two 'Berkano' runes mirrored side by side, representing renewal and vitality.
	Vitality	This complex and powerful bind rune is a combination of 'Ingwaz', fertility, internal growth, 'Berkano', vitality and wellbeing, 'Algiz', protection, 'Uruz', strength and energy.

69

Symbol	Name	Meaning
	Youth and youthfulness	This is a combination of a version of the younger Fuþark rune 'Yr', a yew tree, a symbol of rebirth, and a medieval version of the rune 'Àr' meaning a harvest and a good year.
	Eternal love	This is a combination of 'Gebo', gifts, relationship, partnership, blessing, balance, giving and exchanging, and union, and 'Jera', peace, prosperity, fruitful harvest, and harmony of magical will.
	Charm for a man towards a man	This is a version of 'Ingwaz', representing 'Ing' or 'Yngvi', another name for the god 'Freyr', Norse god of peace and male fertility, bound with 'Isaz', and with all lines reaching outwards.
	Charm for a man towards a woman	A combination 'Tiwaz', honour, the Norse warrior god Tyr, 'Ihwaz', strength, reliability, 'Kenaz', a torch, passion, determination, and the younger Fuþark 'Mathr', man.
	Charm for a woman towards a man	A combination of 'Ingwaz', an opening, love and gentleness, 'Kenaz', a torch, passion, control of sexual energy.

6. Bind Runes

Symbol	Name	Meaning
	Charm for a woman towards a woman	A combination of 'Ingwaz', an opening, love and gentleness, several mirrored 'Berkano' runes for nurturing and fertility magic.
	Love	This is a combination of a version of the younger Fuþark runes 'Yr', a yew tree, a symbol of rebirth, renewal, and trust, and a version of the rune 'As' meaning 'Æsir', the principal pantheon of the Norse gods.
	Good luck and good fortune	This is a combination of the rune 'Gebo', a gift, a blessing, giving and exchanging, and 'Ansuz', meaning 'Æsir', the principal pantheon of the Norse gods.
	Good luck and good fortune	This is a combination of 'Jeran', a good year, peace, prosperity, a fruitful harvest, and 'Isaz' used as a binding rune to hold in place and secure it.
	Good luck and good fortune	This is a combination of the younger Fuþark 'Fe', wealth, luck, energy, foresight, a version of 'Bjarken', new beginnings, and a version of 'As' meaning 'Æsir', the principal pantheon of the Norse gods.

Runes   *6. Bind Runes*

Symbol	Name	Meaning
	Protection against evil magic	This is a combination of 'Ihwaz', a yew tree, strength, reliability, trustworthiness, knowledge, and 'Thurisaz', a thorn, a reactive force, defence, protection, a warning.
	Defence	This is a combination of 'Tiwaz', the Norse warrior god 'Tyr', justice and protection, and heroic glory, and 'Othala', strengthening and connecting with spiritual ancestry, and strengthening and protecting what is yours.
	Elimination of obstacles	This is a combination of 'Ingwaz', meaning an opening or opportunity, bound together with 'Uruz', untamed potential and the strength of a wild ox.
	Protection of home and property	This is a combination of 'Othala', heritage, home, your land of birth, your ancestry, and protection of what is yours, and 'Algiz', a shield, warding off evil, an invisible barrier, giving protection, and strengthening spiritual will.
	Personal protective power	This is a combination of several 'Algiz' runes, spiritual cleansing and connection with a guardian spirit for protection, and 'Ingwaz', for storing and transferring magical power.

Symbol	Name	Meaning
	Return ill will to the originator	This is a combination of 'Hagalaz', used for completeness and bringing into being, and for warding and protection, and a version of 'Sowilo', strengthening magical spiritual will, and success.
	Securing justice	This is a combination of 'Tiwaz', the Norse warrior god 'Tyr', honour, justice, authority, strengthening spiritual and moral force, 'Reith', a spiritual journey, evolution, and planning, bound together with opposing alternative versions of 'Tyr'.
	Protection for a vehicle	This is a combination of 'Algiz' for protection, 'Ihwaz', the yew tree, strength and reliability, trustworthiness, and 'Kenaz', vision and technical ability.
	Protection	This is a combination of 'Algiz', a shield, protection, warding off evil, an impenetrable barrier, and 'Thurisaz', a thorn, a reactive force, warding and defence, changes, and warning, awakening the magical will.
	Assertiveness	This is a combination of 'Tiwaz', Tyr, the Norse warrior god of justice, authority, and heroic glory, and 'Thurisaz', awakening the magical will.

Symbol	Name	Meaning
	Binding power and personal magnetism	This is a combination of the Anglo-Saxon rune 'Stan', meaning stone, 'Iar', strength and reliability, storing power, and 'Nyd', to bind, or hold on to.
	Boosting self esteem	This is a combination of 'Ehwaz', mystical wisdom, projecting and linking magical thoughts, cooperation, and 'Mannaz', strengthening all matters of the mind and psychic ability, balanced through meditation.
	Determination	This is a combination of 'Uruz', strength, untamed potential, 'Nauthiz', self-reliance, overcoming stress, inner might, and 'Ehwaz', a shamanic totem, mystical wisdom, projecting and linking magical thoughts, cooperation.
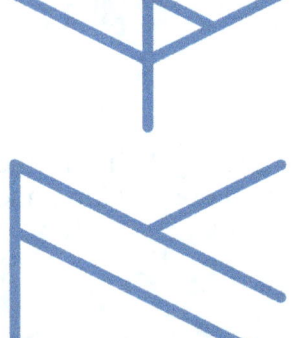	Discipline	This is a combination of the Anglo-Saxon rune 'Jear', meaning strength and reliability, and 'Nyd', holding on to something, binding to something, limitations.
	Discovery of hidden knowledge	This is a combination of 'Perthro', representing mysteries, secrets, the unknown, the occult (that which is hidden), and 'Ansuz', insight, true vision, a secret discovered, finding the truth in the matter.

Symbol	Name	Meaning
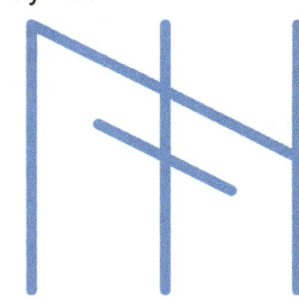	Endurance	This is a combination of 'Uruz', strength, untamed potential, 'Nauthiz', self-reliance, overcoming stress, endurance, and inner might.
	Farsightedness	This is a combination of 'Kenaz', a torch or vision, and 'Algiz', communication and connection with a guardian spirit, travelling through other worlds.
	Following dreams and passions	This is a combination of 'Laguz', representing water, dreams, and fantasies, 'Ihwaz', strength, reliability, slow steady growth, and knowledge, and a version of 'Ingwaz', internal growth, going forward, opening or an opportunity.
	Heart and realising ambition	This is a combination of the younger Fuþark rune 'Reith' two mirrored side by side, representing travel, a journey, and evolution, and 'Nauthir' representing wants and needs, overcoming, developing magical will, inspiration and might.
	Hope	This is a combination of two 'Tiwaz' runes overlapped, the Norse warrior god Tyr, divine justice, authority, honour, and heroic glory, and 'Uruz', healing, shaping and forming of desire or will, with knowledge of the self.

Symbol	Name	Meaning
	Inspiration	This is a combination of 'Laguz', water, dreams, fantasies, probing the subconscious and the unknown, and 'Uruz', healing, shaping and forming of desire or will, and knowledge of the self.
	Music	This is a combination of a version of the younger Fuþark rune 'Yr', a yew tree, a symbol of rebirth, and several overlapping versions of 'As', representing divine communication, and 'Æsir', the principal pantheon of the Norse gods.
	Peace, tranquillity and unity	This is a combination of 'Raido', a spiritual journey, ordered movement, 'Berkano', renewal and nurturing, and 'Laguz', water, going with the flow.
	Perseverance and everlastingness	This is a combination of 'Ingwaz', gestation, internal growth, love, caring, gentleness, storing or transferring magical power, and 'Dagaz', breakthrough, embarking on an enterprise, mystical inspiration.
	Quick results and rapid action	This is a combination of 'Raido', the chariot, travel, evolution, rhythm and timing, movement, and 'Laguz', increasing and filling yourself with life force, physical and magical strength.

Symbol	Name	Meaning
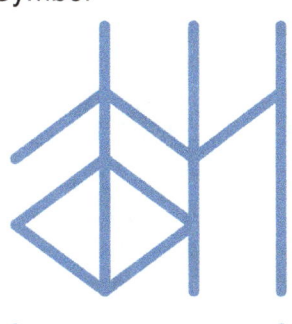	Wisdom	This is a combination of a version of 'Jeran', the yew tree, steady growth of knowledge, 'Sowilo', guidance and triumph, 'Algiz', spiritual cleansing, and connection and communication with a guardian spirit.
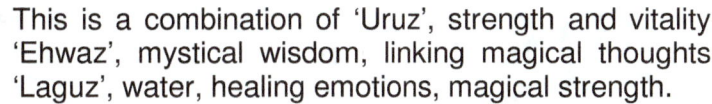	Emotional strength	This is a combination of 'Uruz', strength and vitality, 'Ehwaz', mystical wisdom, linking magical thoughts, 'Laguz', water, healing emotions, magical strength.
	Health & wellbeing	This is a combination of 'Gebo', balance, an endless exchange of energy, and 'Algiz', spiritual cleansing, strengthening magical power, and protection.
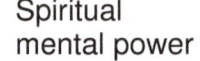	Spiritual and mental power	This is a combination of 'Mannaz', intelligence and confidence, capability, and creative skill, and 'Ansuz', divine communication, and 'Æsir', the principal pantheon of the Norse gods.
	Academic brilliance	This is a combination of two 'Ansuz' runes overlapped, to double this rune's properties of insight, communication, true vision, and finding the truth in the matter. Ansuz also means 'Æsir', the principal pantheon of the Norse gods.

Symbol	Name	Meaning
	Success in exams	This is a combination of 'Mannaz', confidence, intelligence, creative skill, strengthening all matters of the mind, and several versions of a torch 'Kaunan' (Elder Fuþark), 'Kaun' (Younger Fuþark), and 'Cen' (Anglo-Saxon).
	Success in legal matters	This is a combination of 'Raido', moral justice, movement, travel, and 'Tiwaz', the Norse warrior god Tyr, honour, justice, authority, strengthening spiritual and moral force.
	Success in taking risks	This is a combination of the Anglo-Saxon runes 'Peorth', the dice cup, mysteries, secrets, chances and gambles, and 'Jear', prosperity, a fruitful harvest.
	Success in speaking and writing	This is a combination of several versions of the 'Ansuz' rune in different forms, overlapped, side by side, reinforcing the rune's meaning of divine communication with 'Æsir', the principal pantheon of the Norse gods.
	Victory	This is a combination of two overlapping 'Tiwaz' runes, the Norse warrior god 'Tyr', justice and victory, and may also be said to contain overlapping 'Ansuz', divine communication, and 'Æsir', the principal pantheon of the Norse gods.

Symbol	Name	Meaning
	Triumph	This is a combination of three overlapping 'Tiwaz' runes, the Norse warrior god 'Tyr', justice and victory, and may also be said to contain overlapping 'Ansuz', divine communication, and 'Æsir', the principal pantheon of the Norse gods.
	Success	This is a combination of 'Berkano', growth, rebirth, new beginnings, bringing things into being, and 'Jera', prosperity, a fruitful harvest, natural harmony of magical will.
	Safe journey	This is a combination of 'Raido', the chariot, travel, evolution, riding, a spiritual journey, and 'Algiz', protection, a shield, warding off evil, a guardian spirit, spiritual cleansing, travelling through other worlds.
	Safe journey	This is a combination of 'Ehwaz', a horse, transportation, change, physical travel, and 'Algiz', protection, a shield, warding off evil, a guardian spirit, spiritual cleansing, travelling through other worlds.
	Safe journey	This is a combination of 'Ehwaz', a horse, transportation, change, physical travel, and 'Algiz', protection, a shield, a guardian spirit, travelling through other worlds, and 'Uruz', speed, strength, and untamed potential.

Runes   *6. Bind Runes*

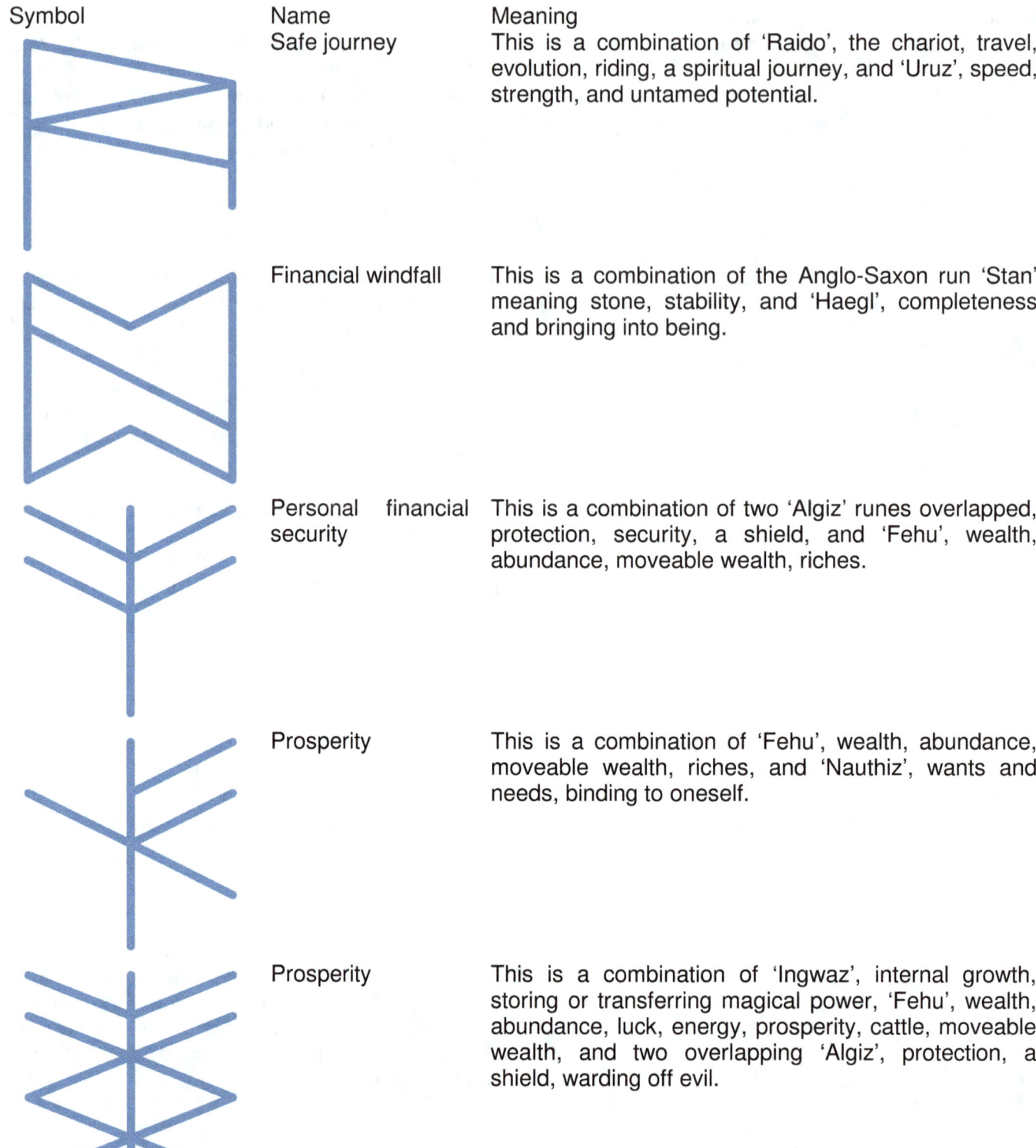

Symbol	Name	Meaning
	Safe journey	This is a combination of 'Raido', the chariot, travel, evolution, riding, a spiritual journey, and 'Uruz', speed, strength, and untamed potential.
	Financial windfall	This is a combination of the Anglo-Saxon run 'Stan' meaning stone, stability, and 'Haegl', completeness and bringing into being.
	Personal financial security	This is a combination of two 'Algiz' runes overlapped, protection, security, a shield, and 'Fehu', wealth, abundance, moveable wealth, riches.
	Prosperity	This is a combination of 'Fehu', wealth, abundance, moveable wealth, riches, and 'Nauthiz', wants and needs, binding to oneself.
	Prosperity	This is a combination of 'Ingwaz', internal growth, storing or transferring magical power, 'Fehu', wealth, abundance, luck, energy, prosperity, cattle, moveable wealth, and two overlapping 'Algiz', protection, a shield, warding off evil.

7. Runic Inscriptions

The surviving runic inscriptions give us a vital source of information about language and social history of the Germanic peoples. The approximate number of known runic inscriptions by area are as follows:

Sweden	3432	Iceland	100
Norway	1552	Continental Europe	80
Denmark	844	Frisia	20
British Isles	200	Ireland	16
Greenland	100	Faeroes	9

It is worth remembering that spelling was not standardised, sometimes letters were left out, and particularly with the Younger Fuþark, one rune could have several different associated sounds.

Rune	Sounds	Rune	Sounds
ᛒ	B / P	ᛁ	I / E / Æ / J
ᛏ	D / T	ᚾ	U / V / O
ᚴ	G / K		Y / Ø / W
ᚠ	F / V	ᛆ	A / Æ
ᚦ	Þ / Ð	ᚮ	A / O / Ö

Words were also abbreviated, and sometimes runes were carved from right to left.

Rune carvings were made by all classes of society, but larger carvings were raised and paid for by the more wealthy, such as earls, chieftains, and kings, etc.

Many rune stones honour the dead, indicate the wealth and authority of those who erected the monuments. Inscriptions also proclaim family relationships, inheritance rights, authority and property claims.

As well as rune stones, inscriptions have also been found on items such as jewellery, weapon parts, knives, spearheads, swords, coins, boxes, containers, bone, pieces of wood, spindles, and even on a cave wall (Kleines Schulerloch inscription, Essing, Bavaria, Germany).

Northumbria, c700s C.E.

Front Panel of the so called 'Franks Casket'
(Source: Wikipedia Creative Commons)

ᚠᛁᛋᚳ.ᚠᛚᚩᛞᚢ.ᚪᚻᚩᚠᚩᚾᚠᛖᚱᚷ	fisc.flodu.ahofonferg |
| ᛖᚾᛒᛖᚱᛁᚷ |	enberig |
ᚹᚪᚱᚦᚷᚪ:ᛋᚱᛁᚳᚷᚱᚩᚱᚾᚦᚫᚱᚻᛖᚩ	warþga:sricgrornþærheo
ᚾᚷᚱᛖᚢᛏᚷᛁᛋᚹᚩᛗ |	ngreutgiswom |
ᚻᚱᚩᚾᚫᛋᛒᚪᚾ	hronæsban

Fisc flōd āhōf on firgenberig. Wearþ gāsric(?) grorn þǣr hē on grēot geswam. Hranes bān.

The flood cast up the fish on the mountain-cliff. The terror-king became sad where he swam on the shingle. Whale's bone.

Jelling, Denmark, c900s C.E.

Gorm's Runestone
(Source: Wikipedia Creative Commons)

: ᚴᚢᚱᛘᛦ : ᚴᚢᚾᚢᚴᛦ :   : kurmʀ : kunukʀ :
: ᚴ(ᛅᚱ)ᚦᛁ : ᚴᚢᛒᛚ : ᚦᚢᛋᛁ :   : k(ar)þi : kubl : þusi :
: ᛅ(ᚠᛏ) : ᚦᚢᚱᚢᛁ : ᚴᚢᚾᚢ   : a(ft) : þurui : kunu
: ᛋᛁᚾᛅ : ᛏᛅᚾᛘᛅᚱᚴᛅᛦ : ᛒᚢᛏ :   : sina : tanmarkaʀ : but :

Gormr konungr gerði kumbl þessi ept þurvi konu sína, Danmarkar bót

King Gormr made this monument in memory of Thyrvé, his wife, Denmark's adornment

Jelling, Denmark, c900s C.E.

Harald's Runestone
(Source: Wikipedia Creative Commons)

ᚼᚱᚭᛚᛏᚱ : ᚴᚢᚾᚢᚴᛦ : ᛒᛅᚦ : ᚴᛅᚢᚱᚢᛅ	haraltr : kunukʀ : baþ : kaurua
ᚴᚢᛒᛚ : ᚦᛅᚢᛋᛁ : ᛅᚠᛏ : ᚴᚢᚱᛘ ᚠᛅᚦᚢᚱ ᛋᛁᚾ	kubl : þausi : aft : kurm faþur sin
ᛅᚢᚴ ᛅᚠᛏ : ᚦᚭᚢᚱᚢᛁ : ᛘᚢᚦᚢᚱ : ᛋᛁᚾᛅ : ᛋᛅ	auk aft : þąurui : muþur : sina : sa
ᚼᚱᚭᛚᛏᚱ (:) ᛁᛅᛋ : ᛋᛅᛦ ᛫ ᚢᛅᚾ ᛫ ᛏᛅᚾᛘᛅᚢᚱᚴ	haraltr (:) ias : saʀ * uan * tanmaurk
ᛅᛚᛅ ᛫ ᛅᚢᚴ ᛫ ᚾᚢᚱᚢᛁᛅᚴ	ala * auk * nuruiak
᛫ ᛅᚢᚴ ᛫ ᛏ(ᛅ)ᚾᛁ (᛫ ᚴᛅᚱᚦᛁ ᛫) ᚴᚱᛁᛋᛏᚾᚭ	* auk * t(a)ni (* karþi *) kristną

Haraldr konungr bað gǫrva kumbl þausi aft Gorm faður sinn auk aft Þórví móður sína. Sá Haraldr es sér vann Danmǫrk alla auk Norveg auk dani gærði kristna

King Haraldr ordered this monument made in memory of Gormr, his father, and in memory of Thyrvé, his mother; that Haraldr who won for himself all of Denmark and Norway and made the Danes Christian

Ramsund, Eskilstuna, Södermanland, Sweden, c1030 C.E.

The Ramsund Carving, Sweden, 11th Century
(Source: Wikipedia Creative Commons)

ᛋᛁᚱᛁᚦᚱ ᚴᛁᛅᚱᚦᛁ ᛒᚢᚱ	siriþr : kiarþi : bur :
ᚦᚭᛋᛁ ᛘᚢᚦᛁᛦ ᛅᛚᚱᛁᚴᛋ	þosi : muþir : alriks :
ᛏᚢᛏᛁᛦ ᚢᚱᛘᛋ ᚠᚢᚱ ᛋᛅᛚᚢ	tutir : urms : fur salu
ᚼᚢᛚᛘᚴᛁᚱᛋ ᚠᛅᚦᛁᚱ	: hulmkirs : faþur :
ᛋᚢᚴᚱᚢᚦᛅᚱ ᛒᚢᛅᛏᛅ ᛋᛁᛋ	sukruþar buata sis

Sigriðr gærði bro þasi, moðir Alriks, dottir Orms, for salu Holmgæirs, faður Sigrøðar, boanda sins

Sigríðr, Alríkr's mother, Ormr's daughter, made this bridge for the soul of Holmgeirr, father of Sigrøðr, her husbandman

Kingittorsuaq, Greenland, c1300s C.E.

The Kingittorsuaq Runestone
(Source: Wikipedia Creative Commons)

el=likr * sikuaþs : so=n:r * ok * baan=ne : torta=r son : ok enriþi * os son : laukardak*in : fyrir * gakndag hloþu * ua=rda te * ok rydu (??????)

Erlingur Sigvaðs sonr og baarne Þorðarson og enriði ás son, laugardagin fyrir gakndag hloðu varða thessa og ryðu (??????)

Erlingur the son of Sigvað and Baarne Þorðar's son and Enriði Ás's son, the washingday (Saturday) before Rogation Day, raised this mound and rode (??????)

8. The Misuse of Runes: What to Avoid

For the last 120 years, runes have been misused, misrepresented, and misinterpreted to fit into systems of propaganda for extreme and objectionable political agendas. This form of cultural appropriation has done great damage in obscuring and twisting the original and true meanings of the runes, to the point where in some landscapes of public consciousness, runes are widely visually associated with Nazism and the horrors of World War 2, Neo-Nazism, far-right extremism, fascism, anti-semitism, racism, white supremacy, and hatred.

The seeds for this deeply problematic offshoot were sown in the early 20th century at a time of heightened nationalism, with a revival of interest in Germanic culture, mythology, runology, and the occult. The Austrian mysticist and Germanic revivalist Guido von List invented and devised the so-called 'Armanen Runes' (Armanen relating to Armanism, Ariosophy, and Aryanism). They consisted of 18 pseudo-runes which were based on the 16 runes of the Younger Futhark with adapted spellings and meanings, and two additional runes loosely based on those from the Anglo-Saxon Futhorc. They were first published in a periodical in 1906, and again as a standalone publication in 1908. The last rune called '*Gibor*' is not related to any historical runes, and is a '*Wolfsangel*' symbol, which particularly in this illustration appears alarmingly similar to the swastika.

ᚠ	fa F	ᚼ	Hagal / Hag H	ᛒ	Bar B
ᚢ	Ur U	ᚾ	Nauth / Not N	ᛚ	Laf L
ᚦ	Thurs Th (Þ)	ᛁ	Is I	ᛘ	Man M
ᚨ	Os A (O)	ᛅ	Ar A	ᛦ	Yr Y
ᚱ	Rit R	ᛋ	Sig / Sol S	ᛖ	Eh E
ᚲ	Ka K	ᛏ	Tyr T		Gibor / Ge / Gi G

Image Source: Wikipedia Creative Commons, Public Domain

The Armanen runes became influential in the Völkisch movement in Germany which promoted interest in Germanic folklore. They had already adopted the swastika as a supposed symbol of Germanic antiquity (a symbol found all over Eurasia as far back as 10,000 BCE, and documented in Sanskrit as far back as 500 BCE), and rejected values such as liberalism, democracy, socialism, and industrial capitalism. They associated these values with the Weimar Republic of Germany which they denounced as being 'un-German' and inspired by subversive Jewish influences. Nazism and Nazi occultism made widespread use of these symbols for propaganda, particularly in the SS (Schutzstaffel) where their use was systematised by Heinrich Himmler. The swastika is still used as a symbol of divinity in Hinduism, Buddhism, and Jainism, but in the western world it will never be able to shake off its association with Nazism, anti-Semitism, white supremacism, and evil.

Since the end of World War 2, continuing efforts have been made by various occultists and runologists to undo the damage done by the Nazi appropriation of runes. These efforts however are undermined by Neo-Nazi movements who have continued to use runes in their propaganda, and as an alternative script for tattoos containing such words and phrases as 'skinhead', 'hate', 'white power', etc. The appearance of runes in this context is understandably visually intimidating to those who cannot read them, and abhorrent to those who can.

In 2019, the government of Sweden discussed the idea of banning the use of runes because of their misappropriation by, and association with such groups. However this would have unfairly punished the far greater number of people who continue to use runes in accordance with the ancient traditions, as spiritual symbols of the interaction of humankind, the forces of nature, the gods, and the universe. It would be a tragedy if we were to relinquish two thousand years of linguistic and spiritual tradition because of the grossly misguided politically motivated actions of a few, the misunderstandings of some, and the lack of knowledge of others. The logic of this debate has also been transposed into a comparative notion of banning the use of the Arabic script because of its use by the militant Islamist group Islamic State (IS).

It is worth noting here which symbols have been misused and how, so that the reader may make careful and informed choices. With the right knowledge they should be well equipped to be able to explain with confidence what their symbol *actually* means, and what it definitely does *not* mean, highlighting the large degree of separation between original and misappropriated meaning. It is also worth noting that in designing the configuration and symmetry of runes that some unintended symbols may be inadvertently made or implied, further to the advice given in the Bindrunes section on Page 11.

Since the reader of this book will no doubt be interested in the full and true history of runes and Nordic symbols and their use for spiritual purposes, the last thing that they would want is to have designed their own rune stave only to have it misinterpreted by people who do not know the full history of the symbols, or worse still to be accused of belonging to a political movement or ideology that they do not belong to and would never wish to. From time to time there may be people who make such accusations or claims, understandably believing that they are actively doing a good thing by calling out evil wherever they see it. If the opportunity for an open and well informed debate and discussion is taken, a bridge of greater knowledge and understanding can be built whereupon it may be understood that the true evil lies in the corruption, distortion, and the taking over of that which is good for the purposes of evil. Context is everything, and half-knowledge is a dangerous thing.

Runes *8. The Misuse of Runes: What to Avoid*

Arrow Cross		The 'Arrow Cross' symbol comes from the Hungarian fascist political party known as the Arrow Cross Party, which was active during 1935-45. Since then, various neo-Nazis and white supremacists have used the symbol. In the United States, the 'Arrow Cross' has been used as the logo for a small Mississippi-based white supremacist group known as the Nationalist Movement (which called the image the 'Crosstar'). **Advice: avoid binding 'Tiwaz' or 'Tyr' runes into a stave with 4 points of symmetry to avoid association with this symbol.**
Eif		The 'Eif' rune is a rotated and reflected version of the 'Eihwaz' rune. During the early years of the SS it was used by Hitler's personal administrators, such as Rudolf Hess. **Advice: avoid turning an 'Eihwaz' rune onto its side to avoid association with this symbol.**
Ger		The 'Ger' rune was used to symbolise the communitarian ideal of the SS. The 11th SS Volunteer Panzergrenadier Division Nordland, a Waffen-SS unit, adopted the rune as a variant of its divisional insignia. **Advice: Avoid making 'Sowilo' runes too square, and make them narrower to avoid association with this symbol, but do not place two side by side.**
Hagal		The Armanen version of the 'Hagal' rune was widely used in the SS for its symbolic representation of 'unshakeable faith' in Nazi philosophy according to Heinrich Himmler put it. It was used in SS weddings as well as on the SS-Ehrenring (death's head ring) worn by members of the SS. The rune was also used as division insignia of the 6th SS Mountain Division Nord. **Advice: lengthen the central stem at the top and the bottom so that the proportions are closer to the 'Haglaz' rune of the Younger Futhark to avoid association with this symbol.**
Heilszeichen	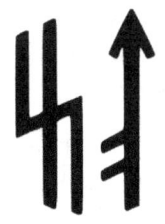	The Heilszeichen symbols appeared on the SS 'death's head' ring and were used to symbolise good fortune and success. **Advice: Avoid making the 'Sowilo' rune too narrow. Do not place two 'Sowilo' runes side by side. Avoid binding an upside down 'Fehu' rune to a 'Tyr' rune to avoid association with this symbol.**

Jera		The 'Jera' rune symbolises concepts such as the harvest or the passage of time. It is one of the less common runic symbols appropriated by modern white supremacists, perhaps because the Nazis do not appear to have used it. In the 2010s, however, white supremacists in Europe and the United States began to use the symbol. In Sweden, for example, the National Youth League (Förbundet Nationell Ungdom), a neo-Nazi group, adopted the Jera rune as its logo. In the United States, the rune began to appear on flyers and cards associated with the alt right segment of the white supremacist movement. Because the Jera rune is used by non-racists as well, including by adherents of modern pagan religions such as Asatru, one should not assume use of the symbol is racist but instead should only judge the symbol carefully in its specific context.
Ku Klux Klan		The triangular Ku Klux Klan symbol consists of what looks like a triangle within a triangle but which actually represents three letter K's aligned in a triangle and facing inwards. The same effect could be inadvertently achieved by creating a triangle of three inward facing 'Berkanaz' runes representing nurturing and motherhood. **Advice: Avoid intersecting lines that result in triangles. Avoid binding runes together with triangular shapes, such as 'Berkanaz' to avoid association with this symbol.**
Leben		The Armanen 'Lebensrune' or 'life rune' was based on the 'Algiz' or 'Elhaz' rune and was used by the Sturmabteilung, NSDAP and the SS. Because of the Nazi use of the symbol, later white supremacists continued to use the Life rune and it became very popular after the neo-Nazi National Alliance adopted the symbol as part of their logo. Since then, it has become a very common white supremacist symbol, used by neo-Nazis and other white supremacists. Because the Life Rune also continues to be used by non-racists, typically adherents of neo-pagan religions, one should not simply assume that a particular use of this symbol is racist, but should carefully judge it in its context.
Opfer		The 'Opfer' rune is a rotated version of the 'Eihwaz' rune. It was used by the Der Stahlhelm war veterans movement that eventually merged with the Sturmabteilung. The symbol was adopted by the Nazis after 1923 to commemorate the party members who died in Hitler's failed Beer Hall Putsch. **Advice: Avoid rotating an 'Eihwaz' rune onto its side to avoid association with this symbol.**

Othala

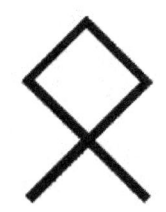

The 'Othala' rune from the Elder Futhark symbolised ancestry, heritage, and family. Its meaning was twisted to mean the protection of ethnic purity. During the Second World War it was used by the SS. Following World War II, white supremacists in Europe, North America, and elsewhere began using the 'Othala' rune. The variation of this rune with additional 'feet' or 'wings' is closely associated with its use by the SS. However, because it is part of the runic alphabet, the symbol can also be found in non-extremist contexts as well, especially runic writing and runestones used by non-racist pagans. Consequently, care should be taken to evaluate the symbol in the context in which it appears.

Both versions of this symbol have been depicted as an astrological symbol for Asteroid #3989 known as 'Odin' discovered on 8th September 1986 by P Jensen at the Brorfelde Observatory in Denmark. The name and number of this asteroid was allocated by the Minor Planet Center (MPC) which is part of the Smithsonian Astrophysical Observatory.

Advice: Avoid using 'feet' or 'wings' for this rune. Even though this variant has been used as an astrological symbol, it is still more closely associated with Nazism than the version without 'feet' or wings'. Its use has also been made illegal in Germany under the 'Strafgesetzbuch section 86a'.

SS Bolts

The SS Bolts are a common white supremacist / neo-Nazi symbol derived from Schutzstaffel (SS) of Nazi Germany. It is derived from the 'Sowilo' or 'sun' rune from the Elder Futhark. Following World War II, the SS bolts symbol was adopted by white supremacists and neo-Nazis worldwide. Most white supremacists use it in its Nazi form, as two bolt-like images with flattened ends. However, sometimes the symbol may have pointed bottom ends or pointed tops and bottoms. These variants of the SS bolts are most frequently associated with prison tattoos. The SS bolts are typically used as a symbol of white supremacy but there is one context in which this is not necessarily always so. Decades ago, some outlaw biker gangs appropriated several Nazi-related symbols, including the SS bolts, essentially as shock symbols or symbols of rebellion or non-conformity. Thus SS bolts in the context of the outlaw biker subculture does not necessarily denote actual adherence to white supremacy. However, because there are a number of racists and full-blown white supremacists within the outlaw biker subculture, sometimes it actually is used as a symbol of white supremacy. Often the intended use and meaning of the SS bolts in this context is quite ambiguous and difficult to determine. **Advice: Avoid placing two 'Sowilo' runes side by side to avoid association with this symbol.**

8. The Misuse of Runes: What to Avoid

Tod

The Todesrune is the inverted version of the Armanen Lebensrune or 'life rune'. It was based on the 'Yr' rune, which originally meant 'yew'. It was used by the SS to represent death on documents and grave markers in place of the more conventional † symbol used for such purposes.

Tyr

The Tyr was based on the 'Tiwaz' rune, named after Týr, the god of single combat, victory and heroic glory in Norse mythology. It was widely used by the SS as a battle rune symbolising military leadership. The SS commonly used it in place of the Christian cross on the grave markers of its members. It was also used by graduates of the SA Reichsführerschule, which trained SS officers until 1934; they wore it on their upper left arms. It was adopted as an emblem by the 32nd SS Volunteer Grenadier Division 30 Januar, which was assembled from the members of SS schools in January 1945, as well as by the SS Recruitment and Training Department. Since World War II, neo-Nazis and other white supremacists continued to use the 'Tyr' rune in a racist context. The Tyr rune is one of the most common white supremacist appropriations of ancient runic symbols. Its popularity in part stems from the fact that it is considered by many to be the 'warrior rune'. Because today the Tyr rune continues to be used by non-racists as well, including members of various neo-pagan religions, one should not assume that use of the symbol is racist but instead should judge the symbol carefully in its specific context.

Valknut

The Valknot or 'knot of the slain' is an old Norse symbol that often represented the afterlife in carvings and designs. It is often considered a symbol of the Norse god Odin. Some white supremacists, particularly racist Odinists, have appropriated the Valknot to use as a racist symbol. Often they use it as a sign that they are willing to give their life to Odin, generally in battle. Non-racist pagans may also use this symbol, so one should carefully examine it in context rather than assume that a particular use of the symbol is racist.

Wolfsangel

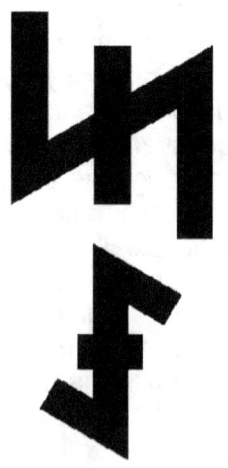

The Wolfsangel is an ancient symbol that was believed to be able to ward off wolves. It appeared as part of the divisional insignia of several Waffen-SS units, including the notorious 2nd SS "Das Reich" Panzer Division. As a result, it became a symbol of choice for neo-Nazis in Europe and the United States. In the United States, the neo-Nazi group Aryan Nations incorporated the Wolfsangel into their logo. **Advice: Avoid inadvertently making or implying this symbol by having any lines intersecting a 'Sowilo' or 'Ihwaz' rune to avoid association with this symbol.**

www.ingramcontent.com/pod-product-compliance
Lightning Source LLC
Chambersburg PA
CBHW051420070526
44584CB00023B/3510